The Ideal Gnome Expedition

A Musical Play

David Wood

A Samuel French Acting Edition

FOUNDED 1830

SAMUELFRENCH-LONDON.CO.UK
SAMUELFRENCH.COM

Copyright © 1982 by David Wood
All Rights Reserved

THE IDEAL GNOME EXPEDITION is fully protected under the copyright laws of the British Commonwealth, including Canada, the United States of America, and all other countries of the Copyright Union. All rights, including professional and amateur stage productions, recitation, lecturing, public reading, motion picture, radio broadcasting, television and the rights of translation into foreign languages are strictly reserved.

ISBN 978-0-573-05061-9

www.samuelfrench-london.co.uk

www.samuelfrench.com

FOR AMATEUR PRODUCTION ENQUIRIES

UNITED KINGDOM AND WORLD EXCLUDING NORTH AMERICA

plays@SamuelFrench-London.co.uk

020 7255 4302/01

Each title is subject to availability from Samuel French, depending upon country of performance.

CAUTION: Professional and amateur producers are hereby warned that *THE IDEAL GNOME EXPEDITION* is subject to a licensing fee. Publication of this play does not imply availability for performance. Both amateurs and professionals considering a production are strongly advised to apply to the appropriate agent before starting rehearsals, advertising, or booking a theatre. A licensing fee must be paid whether the title is presented for charity or gain and whether or not admission is charged.

The professional rights in this play are controlled by Casarotto Ramsay Associates, Waverley House, 7-12 Noel Street, London, W1F 8GQ.

No one shall make any changes in this title for the purpose of production. No part of this book may be reproduced, stored in a retrieval system, or transmitted in any form, by any means, now known or yet to be invented, including mechanical, electronic, photocopying, recording, videotaping, or otherwise, without the prior written permission of the publisher. No one shall upload this title, or part of this title, to any social media websites.

The right of David Wood to be identified as author of this work has been asserted by him in accordance with Section 77 of the Copyright, Designs and Patents Act 1988

THE IDEAL GNOME EXPEDITION

First produced by the Liverpool Playhouse Company under the title *Chish 'n' Fips* on 3rd December, 1980, with the following cast of characters:

Mr Fisher	David Monico
Mr Wheeler	Alan Thompson
Baby Duck	Jane Egan
Chips	Richard Fox
Securidog	Frank Ellis
Wacker	Daniel Webb

Directed by William Gaunt and Peter Lichtenfels
Designed by Bim Hopewell
Choreography by Neil Fitzwiliam
Musical Director Stuart Barham

Subsequently produced at Sadler's Wells Theatre, London and on tour by Whirligig Theatre (sponsored by Clarks Shoes and subsidized by Arts Council Touring) in the autumn of 1981, with the following cast of characters:

Mr Fisher	Mike Elles
Mr Wheeler	Gary Linley
Baby Duck	Melody Kaye
Chips	Keith Varnier
Securidog	Clive Mantle
Wacker	Clive Mantle

Directed by David Wood
Designed by Susie Caulcutt
Choreography by Sheila Falconer
Music arranged and supervised by Peter Pontzen
Musical Director Paul Knight

SCENES

ACT 1
    Scene 1   The Back Yard
    Scene 2   The Alley
    Scene 3   The Adventure Playground

ACT 2
    Scene 1   The Street
    Scene 2   The Island
    Scene 3   The Back Yard

MUSICAL NUMBERS

ACT 1
1. **The Code Of The Gnomes** — Mr Wheeler, Mr Fisher
2. **A Duck Called—?** — Mr Wheeler, Mr Fisher and (Baby Duck)
3. **Holiday Island** — Mr Wheeler, Mr Fisher and (Baby Duck)
4. **This Is My Patch** — Chips
5. **Use Your Eyes and Ears** — Chips, Mr Wheeler, Mr Fisher and (Baby Duck)
6. **A Real Adventure Playground Adventure** — Mr Wheeler, Mr Fisher, Chips and (Baby Duck)
6a. **Holiday Island** (Reprise) — Chips, Mr Wheeler, Mr Fisher and (Baby Duck)

ACT 2
7. **Stuck Duck** — Chips
8. **I'm Wacker!** — Wacker
9. **Sitting Fishing** — Mr Fisher, Mr Wheeler, Chips and (Baby Duck)
9a. **Use Your Eyes and Ears** (Reprise) — Chips, Mr Wheeler, Mr Fisher and (Baby Duck)
9b. **Holiday Island** (Reprise) — Mr Wheeler, Mr Fisher, Chips and (Baby Duck)
10. **Back Home** — Mr Wheeler, Mr Fisher, Chips and (Baby Duck)
10a. **The Code Of The Gnomes** (Reprise) — Mr Wheeler, Mr Fisher

The piano/vocal score is available from Samuel French Ltd

CHARACTERS

Mr Fisher A garden gnome, whose usual function is to sit on a toadstool with his fishing-rod. Rather grumpy and dissatisfied with his lot; nevertheless, like all garden gnomes, he has a warm heart.

Mr Wheeler A garden gnome who is normally to be seen holding his wheelbarrow. Dressed identically to Mr Fisher, he is more of an optimist and an adventurer. Very practical.

NB: Both gnomes have an olde worlde charm and quaint over-polite way of talking to each other and others.

Baby Duck A clockwork toy duck, complete with detachable key sticking out of his back. Could be dressed in a nappy. Waddles slightly stiffly. Cannot talk or sing – only quack. (Could be played by a male or female).

Chips An alley-cat, who has learnt the hard way to survive in the concrete jungle of the town. Knows his way around and how to look after himself. Doesn't easily trust anyone, but once he has accepted someone as a friend, will stick by them. Quite a cool cat!

Securidog Night watchdog at the Adventure Playground. Unnecessarily unpleasant and rude. Also rather stupid. Could be wearing a kind of security officer's uniform or hat.

Wacker A pneumatic machine which bounces up and down flattening uneven road surfaces or tar. As a character he is bouncy and determined to flatten everything in sight – that is, for logical reasons, his reason for living. He should be considerably taller than the others – the actor encased in a high cylinder.

(**Securidog** and **Wacker** could be doubled by the same actor).

Off-Stage (Recorded) voices of the **Big Ones,** the human beings in whose garden/back yard the gnomes live: mother, father and child. Also the voices of two policemen.

PRODUCTION NOTE

Most of the characters in the play would in reality be between eighteen inches and two feet high. Therefore the scale of the settings should be about three or four times "human-size"; i.e., the kerb of the pavement should be, say, two or three feet high; the dustbin, say, six or seven feet high. The environment throughout is urban, but the sets and costumes should still be very colourful and visually exciting.

Much use is made of lighting and sound effects, all of which help create a world in which human activities are seen through the eyes of animals and garden gnomes; so, for instance, the sound of a car and the glare of its headlights will be magnified for these smaller folk.

Photographs of the sets for the Whirligig Theatre production, designed by Susie Caulcutt

Act I, Scene 1 and Act II, Scene 3: The Back Yard

Act 1, Scene 2: The Alley

Act 1, Scene 3: The Adventure Playground

Act 2, Scene 1: The Street

Act 2, Scene 2: The Island

ACT 1

Scene 1

The Back Yard

After a short overture, the House Lights go down, and the CURTAIN *rises on a darkened stage. Over loudspeakers, we hear the sound of a back door being unbolted, top and bottom. Then a key turns in the lock and the door opens. Now we hear the voices of the Big Ones, the human beings whose back yard we are about to visit*

Miss Big One (*who is about eight years old*) But, Mum, it's my favourite.
Mrs Big One I know, love, but it's broken.
Miss Big One (*shouting*) Then mend it.
Mrs Big One Don't talk to me like that. Your dad's tried to mend it, but he can't. He's going to buy you a new one.
Miss Big One I don't *want* a new one.
Mrs Big One Don't be silly.
Miss Big One I want this one.
Mrs Big One But it's broken. It's useless.
Miss Big One But, Mum ...

We hear a dustbin lid being removed, the metallic clang of something being thrown in, and finally the lid slammed back down

(*Shrieking*) Mum! (*She starts crying*)

Mrs Big One (*briskly*) Come on. Inside. I've had enough.

We hear the slam of the back door as the Big Ones return inside

Music as the Lights go up on a corner of a back yard or urban back garden

A wall: on it a tap with an attached hosepipe coiled round it. Maybe a flower-bed or a couple of tubs with plants in. A dustbin, the lid half on, half off. In prominent positions we see two garden gnomes, identically dressed. Mr Fisher sits crosslegged on a stone toadstool; he holds a fishing-rod. Mr Wheeler stands next to the toadstool. He holds his wheelbarrow. Both Gnomes are in frozen positions. Mr Fisher is asleep. Other items of garden/back yard dressing could be visible, and it might be effective if the Gnomes were on a small patch of grass. But it is important that the garden/back yard is noticeably urban rather than rural. We imagine that the back door is off-stage, to one side or out front, in the audience as it were. It is afternoon

From the dustbin we hear a sort of quacking cry for help. Once. Twice. On the third cry, Mr Wheeler "comes to life". He registers concern, checks that nobody is coming, leaves his wheelbarrow and scuttles over to the dustbin. He listens, ear against the side. Another quacking cry. Mr Wheeler nips back and looks up at Mr Fisher

Mr Wheeler (*in an urgent whisper*) Mr Fisher!

No reaction

  Mr Fisher!

A loud snore from Mr Fisher. Mr Wheeler tries another tack. He pulls gently on the fishing line; this rings a little bell on the top of the rod. Another snore. Another ring. Another snore. Another ring – more vehement. This time Mr Fisher wakes up with a violent start.

Mr Fisher A bite! A bite! Heave! Heave! Come on, my beauty!

Mr Wheeler is still holding on to the line and is nearly pulled off his feet as Mr Fisher pulls and tugs

Mr Wheeler Mr Fisher!
Mr Fisher My, it's a big 'un. A codfish at least! Heave!
Mr Wheeler Mr Fisher!

He lets go of the line, making Mr Fisher nearly fall off his toadstool

Mr Fisher Aaaah! (*Regaining his balance*) Oh, it's you, Mr Wheeler. I thought you were a codfish.
Mr Wheeler Do I look like a codfish, Mr Fisher?
Mr Fisher (*disappointed*) I must have been dreaming.
Mr Wheeler Do I have a face like a codfish?
Mr Fisher How do I know? I've never seen a codfish face, have I? Or a codfish fin. Or a codfish fillet. Or a codfish finger. I've never seen a *fish*!
Mr Wheeler Please, Mr Fisher, don't start all that again ...
Mr Fisher What a joke! Stuck up here year after year, fishing-rod in fist, with no hope of usefully employing it. My life, Mr Wheeler, is a wasted life.
Mr Wheeler Fiddle faddle, Mr Fisher. I've a job for you and your fishing-rod right now. Listen.

Another quacking cry from the dustbin

Mr Fisher (*with a jump*) What was that?
Mr Wheeler An SOS call. From the dustbin.

Dramatic chord

Mr Fisher The dustbin?

Another quacking cry

Mr Wheeler Something needs our help. Come down, please.
Mr Fisher No, no, no. Leave it there, Mr Wheeler. If the Big Ones throw something away, that's their business. Not ours. If something doesn't work; if it's useless—good riddance.

Act 1, Scene 1 3

Mr Wheeler The Big Ones may throw *you* away one day. Mr Fisher.
Mr Fisher Me?
Mr Wheeler And if they do, I won't lift a finger to rescue you.
Mr Fisher (*nervously*) Why should they throw me away?
Mr Wheeler (*imitating Mr Fisher*) "If something doesn't work" ... "If it's useless" ... Well, *you* don't work ... "My life, Mr Wheeler, is a wasted life" ... (*Pointedly*) Good riddance to *you*.

Another quacking cry. Mr Fisher looks guilty

And besides, Mr Fisher ...
Mr Fisher (*uncomfortable*) Besides, Mr Wheeler?
Mr Wheeler (*significantly*) The Code of the Gnomes.

SONG 1: **The Code Of The Gnomes**

(*Singing*)	If anyone's in trouble or in a mess
	If anyone's unhappy, unwell or in distress
	It's up to us
Mr Fisher (*reluctantly*)	It's up to us?
Mr Wheeler	It's up to us
Mr Fisher (*nodding*)	It's up to us
Mr Wheeler	With no fuss
	It's up to us
	To help him on his way
	It's up to us
Mr Fisher (*getting more enthusiastic*)	It's up to us
Mr Wheeler	It's up to us
Mr Fisher (*whole-heartedly*)	It's up to us
Both	The Code of the Gnomes
	We must obey.

Mr Fisher climbs down from his toadstool

	If ever you're in danger or need a friend
	Be sure that we'll stick by you until the bitter end
Mr Wheeler	It's up to us
Mr Fisher	It's up to us
Mr Wheeler	It's up to us
Mr Fisher	It's up to us
Both	We won't wait
	Or hesitate
	Just put us to the test
Mr Wheeler	It's up to us
Mr Fisher	It's up to us
Mr Wheeler	It's up to us
Mr Fisher	It's up to us

Both The Code of the Gnomes
We do our best.

Gnomes know no
Other way to live
No gnome's slow
His help to give
The Gnomes' Code
Is share the load
And help one another
Along life's road.

Mr Wheeler It's up to us
Mr Fisher It's up to us
Mr Wheeler It's up to us
Mr Fisher It's up to us
Both We won't wait
Or hesitate
Just put us to the test
Mr Wheeler It's up to us
Mr Fisher It's up to us
Mr Wheeler It's up to us
Mr Fisher It's up to us
Both The Code of the Gnomes
We do our best.
It's up to us
It's up to us
It's up to us
It's up to us
The Code of the Gnomes
U.P.T.O.U.S.
Up to us
It's up to us
To do our best.

The music continues as Mr Wheeler gives Mr Fisher a leg-up to the top of the dustbin. If necessary, they use the toadstool or the wheelbarrow to achieve extra height. Mr Fisher peers down inside

Mr Wheeler Well?
Mr Fisher Can't see a thing.

Another quacking cry. Mr Fisher jumps. The Gnomes nearly lose their balance

(*Calling down*) We're going to get you out. Don't move. Stay there.
Mr Wheeler I don't think it has much choice, Mr Fisher.

Music as Mr Fisher tries, unsuccessfully, to reach whatever it is out of the dustbin. Both Gnomes think; then Mr Fisher points to his fishing-rod. Mr Wheeler passes it to him. Carefully he lowers the line into the dustbin. Tension

Act 1, Scene 1

music as the line tightens. After a struggle, he manages to pull up and help out Baby Duck, who is virtually lifeless, though emitting the odd quack. Mr Wheeler helps him to the ground. Both Gnomes hold him up. Thinking he is balanced, they let go of him. He totters and nearly falls. The Gnomes catch him. Then balance him and leave go. Again he nearly falls. This time they hold on to him

Mr Wheeler What it is?
Mr Fisher No idea.
Mr Wheeler (*to the audience*) Maybe you can help. Do you know what this is?
Audience A duck.
Mr Wheeler A what?
Audience A duck.
Mr Fisher Of course! A duck. A baby duck, by the look of it.
Mr Wheeler (*noticing the key sticking out of Baby Duck's back*) What's this?
Mr Fisher A key.
Mr Wheeler But what's it for? (*To the audience*) Do you know? What's the key for?
Audience To wind it up.
Mr Wheeler To what?
Audience To wind it up.
Mr Fisher Of course! It's a toy, Mr Wheeler. You wind it up and it comes to life, I bet.
Mr Wheeler Shall I try it?
Mr Fisher Why not?

Mr Wheeler tries to turn the key

Mr Wheeler It won't budge. It's stuck.
Mr Fisher Why? (*To the audience*) Why?
Audience It's broken.
Mr Fisher Broken? Of course! That's why the Big Ones threw Baby Duck away. He doesn't work.

A weak quacking cry. Baby Duck starts falling forwards in a faint. The Gnomes catch him

Mr Wheeler He's very weak, Mr. Fisher.
Mr Fisher (*idea*) A drink of water.
Mr Wheeler The tap!

They start to carry him. He is heavy

Wheelbarrow.

They tip him into the wheelbarrow and wheel him to the tap and hose

Carry on, Mr Fisher. Back in a jiff.
Mr Fisher Right, Mr Wheeler.

Mr Wheeler exits

Mr Fisher reaches up for the hose and positions it near Baby Duck's mouth. Then he stretches to the tap and turns it very slightly, then turns it off again. He returns to the end of the hose and shakes a drop or two into Baby Duck's mouth

> There. Just a drop.

Baby Duck utters a spluttering quack

> It's all right. Keep calm. We're only trying to help you.

Mr Wheeler returns carrying a large (for him) screwdriver

Mr Wheeler Found this in the Big Ones' shed.

Tension music as Mr Wheeler "operates" on the key area. He carefully twiddles the screwdriver. After a few seconds of concentration ...

> There.

Mr Fisher gently pulls a dirty piece of fluff from the key area

Mr Fisher Ugh. No wonder.

Tension music continues as the Gnomes carefully tip Baby Duck from the wheelbarrow. Mr Wheeler gingerly turns the key. A ratchet noise indicates it is now turning. Several turns. Then the Gnomes stand to one side and eagerly watch. Slowly a very excited Baby Duck comes to life and then starts waddling fast and furiously. The Gnomes have, perhaps, to jump out of his way. Joyfully he scuttles around exploring, then returns to the Gnomes to thank them for mending him, all the time quacking with delight. He bows up and down several times

> What's he doing?

Mr Wheeler Saying thank you. Our pleasure, Baby Duck, our pleasure.

Now Baby Duck starts to run down. His movements become slow and jerky until he stops altogether

Mr Fisher Has he conked out again?
Mr Wheeler No. Just needs rewinding.

Ratchet noises as he does so. Baby Duck comes to life again. He smiles at the Gnomes

> Now, let's say hello properly.

Mr Fisher Is that his name?
Mr Wheeler What?
Mr Fisher Properly. Funny name for a duck.
Mr Wheeler No. Let's say hello properly. Introduce ourselves. Hello. (*He bows*)

Baby Duck quacks and bows

Act 1, Scene 1   7

I'm Mr Wheeler. This is Mr Fisher.
Mr Fisher bows. Baby Duck bows
Mr Fisher How do you do?
Baby Duck quacks
What's *your* name?
Baby Duck shrugs
You don't know?
Baby Duck shrugs again
You haven't got a name?
Baby Duck shakes his head
Mr Wheeler. He hasn't got a name.
Mr Wheeler That'll never do. Everyone should have a name.
Baby Duck indicates the audience
What?
Baby Duck indicates the audience and quacks again
Ask *them* to think of a name for you?
Baby Duck nods
Good idea. Anyone got a good name for a baby duck?
Audience participation: the Gnomes invite suggested names. After rejecting a couple, Baby Duck nods his acceptance of one. For the purposes of the script, let's call him "Fluffy"
He likes it! (*To the audience*) Thank you. Fluffy Duck!

SONG 2: **A Duck Called——?**

Mr Fisher ⎫   Once there was a duck called Fluffy
Mr Wheeler ⎭   Went and got a bit of fluff in his works
With a worried frown
This duck ran down
In a flurry of jiggles and jerks.

But
Fluffy
Your problems are ended
Fluffy
You can waddle and quack
Fluffy
Your clockwork is mended
Fluffy
Welcome back.

Fluffy
Your problems . . .

Mr Wheeler Wait a minute! Mr Fisher, I have an excellent idea.
Mr Fisher Carry on, Mr Wheeler
Mr Wheeler (*taking in the audience*) Since *they* thought of the name "Fluffy", why don't they join in the song? Would you do that?
Audience Yes.
Mr Wheeler Would you?
Audience Yes.
Mr Wheeler Splendid. Every time the word "Fluffy" crops up in the song, you shout it out. (*Demonstrating*) Fluffy! Yes? Have a go now. After three. One, two, three.
Audience Fluffy!
Mr Wheeler Excellent!
Mr Fisher Mr Wheeler, I have an idea too.
Mr Wheeler Carry on, Mr Fisher.
Mr Fisher To give them a signal every time the word "Fluffy" comes up, I'll lift my fishing-rod high in the air.
Mr Wheeler Good.
Mr Fisher Let's try it. Here we go. One, two, three. (*He raises his fishing-rod*)
Audience Fluffy!
Mr Fisher And again!

Into the song ...

Audience	Fluffy
Mr Fisher / **Mr Wheeler**	Your problems are ended
Audience	Fluffy
Mr Fisher / **Mr Wheeler**	You can waddle and quack
Audience	Fluffy
Mr Fisher / **Mr Wheeler**	Your clockwork is mended
Audience	Fluffy
Mr Fisher / **Mr Wheeler**	Welcome back! Once there was a duck called
Audience	Fluffy
Mr Fisher / **Mr Wheeler**	In the bin the Big Ones threw him away But we heard him shout And fished him out So he'd live to see another day. So
Audience	Fluffy
Mr Fisher / **Mr Wheeler**	Your problems are ended
Audience	Fluffy
Mr Fisher / **Mr Wheeler**	You can waddle and quack

Act 1, Scene 1

Audience	Fluffy
Mr Fisher ⎫ **Mr Wheeler** ⎭	Your clockwork is mended
Audience	Fluffy
Mr Fisher ⎫ **Mr Wheeler** ⎭	Welcome back!
All	Fluffy!

The music continues. They dance happily. Then, suddenly, we hear loud noises of the Big Ones. Bolts being undone, key turning and the back door opening. A dramatic lighting change—perhaps human shadows towering over the characters on stage

Immediately the two Gnomes expertly rush back to their places. If necessary, they drag the toadstool back in place. Mr Fisher retrieves his fishing-rod and climbs back up. Mr Wheeler grabs his wheelbarrow. Baby Duck, unused to this ritual, stands uneasily. Mr Fisher and Mr Wheeler beckon or usher him to a position of safety—out of sight of the Big Ones. Behind the toadstool, perhaps. Baby Duck pops out again

Mr Wheeler Back, Fluffy Duck, back.

Baby Duck obeys. Mr Fisher and Mr Wheeler freeze

The voices of the Big Ones boom out

Miss Big One Come on. Granny will think we're never coming.
Mrs Big One Have we got everything?
Mr Big One Everything but the kitchen sink. Anyone would think we were going for six months, not just a weekend.

We hear the door shutting, and the key turning

Mrs Big One I've cancelled the milk, turned off the gas, shut the windows...
Miss Big One Come on, Mum.
Mr Big One Hey! Who's been playing around with my screwdriver?

The Gnomes exchange worried expressions. They haven't had time to return the screwdriver to the shed. Tension music

Miss Big One Not me.
Mrs Big One Not me.
Mr Big One I wish people would put things back where they found them. I s'pose *I'll* have to.
Miss Big One Come on, Dad. We're late.
Mr Big One Oh, all right. (*Tutting noise*) Bet it gets all rusty.

We hear the sound of car doors slamming, the engine starting and the car driving off

The lighting returns to normal. The Gnomes unfreeze

Mr Wheeler All clear, Fluffy Duck. They've gone.

Baby Duck emerges

Mr Fisher Trust him to notice that screwdriver.
Mr Wheeler My fault for leaving it there.
Mr Fisher The Big Ones notice everything.
Mr Wheeler At least they didn't notice Fluffy Duck wasn't in the dustbin.

Baby Duck quacks

Mr Fisher My nerves won't stand it, Mr Wheeler. Being taken by surprise like that. Why can't they leave us in peace?
Mr Wheeler They have. For the weekend, anyway. Didn't you hear, Mr Fisher? They've gone to see Granny. We're free! Free to do as we please.
Mr Fisher Well, I shall go back to sleep. That will please me.
Mr Wheeler No! This is a time for excitement! Adventure! Doing things we always wanted to do.
Mr Fisher What things?
Mr Wheeler Fishing! You've always wanted to fish.
Mr Fisher I've never seen a fish. Fish don't live in back yards.
Mr Wheeler Exactly. We'll go away. On holiday. For the weekend. Like the Big Ones. What do you say, Fluffy Duck?

Baby Duck quacks

Mr Fisher (*getting interested*) I once heard the Big Ones talk of things called "islands". It seems islands are holiday places in the sun, surrounded by sea water. Water in which fish swim. Hundreds and thousands of fish.
Mr Wheeler We'll find an island, then. (*Reaching up to Mr Fisher on his toadstool*) Come on.
Mr Fisher But, Mr Wheeler, we've never left the back yard before. Who knows what dangers lie beyond that wall?
Mr Wheeler Who knows indeed, Mr Fisher? But we'll soon find out.

SONG 3: **Holiday Island**

(*Singing*) Ev'ryone needs a change of scene
Including you and me
Year after year
We've not moved from here
Now is our chance to be free.

Mr Fisher smiles and nods his agreement

Mr Wheeler
Mr Fisher } So
Let's find our holiday island
Our holiday yours and my land
Where there's nothing to do
But enjoy doing nothing
Where there's nothing to do
But have fun
Let's find our holiday yours and my land
Island in the sun.

Act 1, Scene 2

Mr Fisher A quiet spot
Where a quiet spot of fishing
Would make my wishing
Come true
Mr Wheeler ⎫ Far away
Mr Fisher ⎭ A place to play
Where the sky is always blue.

Mr Wheeler and Mr Fisher, carried away by their thoughts, stop singing and gaze ahead in reverie. Baby Duck quacks to "awaken" them

Baby Duck Quack, quack, quack.
Mr Wheeler ⎫ Let's find our holiday island
Mr Fisher ⎭ Our holiday pie in the sky land
If we're feeling too warm
We can splash in the water
Then get dry in the sun's golden beams
Let's find our holiday yours and my land
Pie in the sky land
Do or die land
Island of our dreams.

They start preparing to go as the music continues. They go to the wall, throw the hose up and over the wall, like a rope. Mr Wheeler, using the tap as a foothold, scrambles up. Mr Fisher hands him his wheelbarrow; or they use the hose to lift it. Then Mr Fisher hands up his fishing-rod. Helped by Mr Wheeler, Mr Fisher uses the tap and hose to climb up. Finally, Baby Duck, maybe reluctantly at first, climbs up. All three are now on top of the wall

Let's find our holiday yours and my land
Pie in the sky land
Do or die land
Island in the sun.

They disappear over the wall. (N.B. Mr Fisher leaves behind his fishing-rod)

The Lights fade to a Black-out

Scene 2

The Alley

This will most easily be a simple front cloth—in order to cover the scene change. It represents a wall, colourfully vandalized with graffiti or posters, spray paints, chalked cricket stumps, etc. (In one production of the play, the "back yard" set was two revolving trucks, on the other side of which were the two sections of wall). Downstage is a street-lamp—just the upright part; the lamp itself is out of view, up in the flies; it is not turned on yet. It is dusk

From the shadows, or over the wall, Chips enters, on the prowl. He sniffs around hungrily

SONG 4: **This Is My Patch**

Chips
When I'm out on the prowl
The other cats all fly
They wouldn't stop and sniff me
They wouldn't dare to try
No, *no* cat muscles in on me
'Cos I'm the Boss round here
And I can scratch—
This is my patch

Though I look sort of scruffy
Up top I'm sort of smart
The struggle for survival
Is really quite an art
So don't come interfering when
I'm scavenging for scraps
Don't try to snatch—
This is my patch.

Some cats
Lead a life of luxury
Cuddly and clean and pretty
But an alley cat
Can't be a pally cat
When he's starving
In the streets of the city.

Some nasty kids once caught me
And flung me down a hole
I've had to learn the hard way
So I don't trust a soul
Right now I'm on the look out for
A juicy bite to eat
A tasty catch
May meet its match
On this—my patch.

As the song ends, Chips reacts to a voice off-stage

Mr Wheeler (*off*) Forward, Mr Fisher. This way.

Chips beats a hasty retreat

From the other side, Mr Wheeler enters pushing the wheelbarrow. Baby Duck is inside, asleep. Mr Fisher follows a few paces behind. He is tired

Mr Fisher Oooh! My legs.
Mr Wheeler Ssh, Mr Fisher, *please*. Fluffy Duck's asleep. He's had a nerve-wracking day.
Mr Fisher *He's* had a nerve-wracking day. *My* nerves have never been so wracked. I'm exhausted.
Mr Wheeler Let's have a rest then.

Act 1, Scene 2

They stop under the street-lamp. Mr Wheeler sits on his barrow

Mr Fisher (*sitting down*) Ohhh! I wasn't made for walking. I was made for sitting cross-legged. That's better.
Mr Wheeler What an exciting journey. Aren't you glad we came, Mr Fisher?
Mr Fisher I just hope it's safe here. It's getting quite dark.

A sudden burst of light hits them from above, making them jump

Jumping toadstools! What's that?
Mr Wheeler Lightning! Look out for the thunder!

They both cover their ears and close their eyes. Nothing happens. After a short while, they peep

Mr Fisher Can't have been lightning. Didn't flash. Still here, look.
Mr Wheeler What is it then? (*To the audience*) Anybody know?
Audience A street-lamp.
Mr Wheeler A what?
Audience A street-lamp.

Mr Wheeler looks up

Mr Wheeler Of course. Look, Mr Fisher. This is a special lamp—it lights up the street when it gets dark.
Mr Fisher How very thoughtful, I feel much safer now. Good-night, Mr Wheeler. (*He settles in his usual cross-legged position*).
Mr Wheeler Good-night, Mr Fisher.
Mr Fisher (*suddenly*) Aaaaaaah!
Mr Wheeler Quiet, please. You'll wake Fluffy Duck.
Mr Fisher It's gone. It's gone.
Mr Wheeler No, it hasn't. It's in the wheelbarrow.
Mr Fisher Not Fluffy Duck, you noodly gnome. My fishing-rod! My fishing-rod! (*He jumps up and searches*)
Mr Wheeler Stop flappety flapping, Mr Fisher. Where is it?
Mr Fisher If I knew where it was, I wouldn't be flappety flapping, would I? I've lost it.
Mr Wheeler You must have left it behind.
Mr Fisher Behind what?
Mr Wheeler Not behind what. Behind. Back in the back yard.
Mr Fisher Then back we must go for it, Mr Wheeler.
Mr Wheeler We can't go back now.
Mr Fisher I insist.
Mr Wheeler You go back.
Mr Fisher On my own? Certainly not. You come too.
Mr Wheeler All that way? Just for a fishing-rod?
Mr Fisher Just for a fishing-rod? Mr Wheeler, my fishing-rod is all I have in the whole world.
Mr Wheeler Oh, very well. What about Fluffy Duck?
Mr Fisher Leave him here. He's fast asleep. We won't be long.
Mr Wheeler But my wheelbarrow ... Oh, I suppose it'll be all right. (*To the audience*) Will you keep an eye out for us, please?

Audience Yes.
Mr Wheeler Thank you. Thank you very much.
Mr Fisher (*impatient*) Come on, Mr Wheeler.

They scuttle off

Tension music as, from the other side, Chips enters. He hungrily approaches the barrow, licking his lips when he sees Baby Duck inside

The Audience may well shout a warning. Just as Chips goes to pounce, Baby Duck wakes and sits up in the barrow with a loud quack

Thus taken by surprise, Chips dashes off, or behind the wall

Baby Duck looks around for the Gnomes. He climbs out of the wheelbarrow and looks off-stage. He waddles towards the exit opposite to the one Chips has just left by. He looks off. Turns to the audience and shakes his head—nobody there. He starts waddling back towards the centre

Just behind him, echoing his movement, comes Chips (having run round behind the front cloth or wall)

The audience should shout a warning. Baby Duck realizes something is amiss, stops and turns suddenly. But Chips does exactly the same, running round behind Baby Duck, unseen. This can be repeated. Then Baby Duck turns, sees Chips, who goes to grab him. Baby Duck neatly side-steps, and Chips crashes to the ground. Furious, he gets up and pursues Baby Duck. This becomes a chase—round the street-lamp a couple of times, round or over the barrow; perhaps Baby Duck side-steps the barrow, leaving Chips to fall over it. As Chips lies headlong, Baby Duck suddenly and dramatically starts to run down. Music echoes his struggling helplessness; almost in slow motion his limbs stretch hopelessly. Chips sees his chance, and, rubbing his paws with glee, advances menacingly, preparing to pounce

In the nick of time, the Gnomes enter, returning with Mr Fisher's fishing-rod

The audience may well shout out to them directing them to help Baby Duck, but in any event, they speedily size up the situation, and wade in to help. They get the fishing-rod between Baby Duck and Chips, then drag Chips away, perhaps forcing him to stumble backwards into the wheelbarrow. Mr Fisher stands guard over him, while Mr Wheeler goes to Baby Duck and re-winds him. He "wakes up" again and quacks his gratitude The music ends

(*Prodding Chips with his fishing-rod*) Now then.
Chips Easy, man, easy.
Mr Fisher Easy? What do you mean, easy?
Chips Cool it.
Mr Fisher Cool it? Cool what?
Chips Just cool it. And blow.
Mr Fisher Blow?
Chips Blow.
Mr Fisher Mr Wheeler, I need your assistance.

Mr Wheeler and Baby Duck approach

Act 1, Scene 2   15

Mr Wheeler Yes, Mr Fisher?
Mr Fisher This cat's talking fiddle-faddle. He says I have to cool something by blowing on it. He says it's easy.
Mr Wheeler Explain yourself.
Chips Like there's nothing to explain man.
Mr Wheeler There most certainly is. Why were you attacking this defenceless duck?
Chips He looked sort of yummy.
Mr Wheeler Yummy?
Chips Scrummy.
Mr Wheeler Scrummy?
Chips Out of sight.
Mr Wheeler But how could he look—er—yummy and scrummy if he was out of sight?
Mr Fisher He talks fiddle-faddle. I told you.
Chips He looked good enough to eat. Get it?
Mr Fisher Eat? You wanted to eat him?
Chips Did you think I wanted to dance with him? I'm starving.
Mr Wheeler But you couldn't eat *him*?
Chips You want to bet?

He advances towards Baby Duck, who quacks and backs away

Mr Wheeler But he's not a *real* duck. He's a toy.

Chips stops

Chips Huh?
Mr Wheeler He's a toy.
Chips You mean, one of those clockwork jobs?
Mr Wheeler Yes.
Chips *(philosophically)* Story of my life. Win some, lose some. (*Paw outstretched, he approaches Baby Duck*) Sorry, Duck. Nothing personal.

Baby Duck is unsure and doesn't reciprocate

  Sorry, gents.
Mr Wheeler Gnomes, actually. Mr Fisher. (*He bows*)
Mr Fisher Mr Wheeler. (*He bows*)
Chips Chips.
Mr Wheeler I beg your pardon?
Chips That's what they call me. Chips.
Mr Fisher Funny name for a cat.
Chips That's all he had left.
Mr Fisher Eh?
Chips The guy at the fish and chip shop. Like one day I went and begged for some fish. But he'd sold it all. Only had chips left. I was so hungry, I ate them. So people call me Chips. Well, I'd better blow—(*seeing the Gnomes don't understand*)—er, go.
Mr Wheeler Where are you—er, blowing to? Where do you live?

Chips Here. This alley is my home. This street is my home. This city is my home. Like I'm free. No ties, man. No responsibilities.
Mr Fisher No food...
Chips I get by.
Mr Fisher If only I could catch you a fish—all my life I've wanted to—here's my rod, you see—listen, if I ever catch one, *you* shall have it.
Chips Good on you, Mr Fisher, that's ace, really. Ace.
Mr Fisher I don't know a fish called ace; a plaice, maybe?
Mr Wheeler And who knows? Mr Fisher may catch it very soon. We're on holiday, you see, Chips...

Music for tension. Chips suddenly changes. He shakes with fear and anger

Chips Holiday? Holiday? Horrid things, holidays. I hate them. I hate them.
Mr Wheeler But why? Holidays are for enjoying.
Chips Not when you're left behind, they're not. Like I lived in a house once, with a family of Big Ones; they went on holiday. Like I never saw them again.
Mr Fisher You mean they just left you? Without food or shelter?
Chips They even nailed up the cat flap.
Mr Fisher That's disgraceful.
Chips Mm. Maybe. I don't care. All I know is that now I only have to hear the word "holiday" and I freak out. My whiskers tremble and my fur stands on end.
Mr Wheeler I'm so sorry. I should never have mentioned hol— well, you know—that word.
Chips That's OK, man. You weren't to know. So where are you heading?
Mr Wheeler To be honest, we don't really know.
Mr Fisher We've never left the back yard before.
Chips Well, why don't I show you around? I'll take you anywhere you want. I know this city like the back of my paw.
Mr Wheeler (*uncertain*) Well, that's most kind...

Baby Duck quacks, alarmed

What's the matter, Fluffy Duck?

Baby Duck mimes he isn't sure whether Chips' presence would be a good idea

I'm sure Chips won't hurt you now.

Baby Duck still looks concerned. Mr Wheeler turns to Chips

Well, maybe...
Mr Fisher It might be sensible——
Mr Wheeler —to, er, press on alone.
Chips Don't trust me, huh?
Mr Wheeler It's not that, we —oh, dear, have we hurt your feelings?
Chips No skin off my nose. But I tell you straight. The city's not safe to explore on your tod. You won't get far through the concrete jungle by yourselves. Still. Up to you. Good luck. See you. (*He casually leans against the streetlamp to watch them go*)

The Gnomes are a little uncomfortable, but decide to go

Act 1, Scene 2   17

Mr Wheeler Goodbye.
Mr Fisher Goodbye.

Baby Duck quacks "Goodbye". Music as they prepare to go—collecting wheelbarrow and rod. They start off towards the audience. Sudden frightening light hits their faces, accompanied by a loud noise of a car roaring past. The Gnomes and Baby Duck react terrified, and back away. After a moment to recover they gingerly set off again. Another dazzling light blinds them and another car roars past. Again the Gnomes and Baby Duck recoil, frightened. Chips remains impassive, watching from the street-lamp. Baby Duck quacks in alarm

What's happening, Mr Wheeler?
Mr Wheeler I wish I knew, Mr Fisher.

Baby Duck quacks and points to the audience

What? Ask them? Good idea. (*To the audience*) Do you know what's making all that noise and shining that light?
Audience Cars.
Mr Wheeler I beg your pardon?
Audience Cars.
Mr Fisher Of course, Mr Wheeler. Cars—like the Big Ones' car. Big dangerous things that move very fast.
Mr Wheeler (*to the audience*) Thank you. Would you be kind enough to let us know if another's coming?
Audience Yes.
Mr Wheeler Thanks. Come on, Fluffy. Come on, Mr Fisher.

There is the noise of an approaching vehicle as the three creep forward. The audience shout out a warning. The car flashes by. The Gnomes and Baby Duck look relieved.

(*To the audience, as they move off*) Thanks.

They try again. Another vehicle is heard approaching. Again the Audience shouts out a warning. The Gnomes and Baby Duck stop again in the nick of time. The light hits their faces

Thanks again.
Mr Fisher Mr Wheeler, this is absurd. We'll be here for ever.

Baby Duck quacks and indicates, with a little embarrassment, the impassive Chips

What? Ask Chips to help? Trust him?

Baby Duck nods

Mr Fisher I agree. Mr Wheeler?
Mr Wheeler So do I, but we may well have upset Chips by turning down his offer the first time. Let's try, anyway.

They go back to Chips

Er ... Chips.
Chips Mmmmm?
Mr Wheeler We—er ...

Chips Mmmmm?

Baby Duck quacks, apologizing

Mr Wheeler Fluffy Duck apologizes. We all apologize.
Mr Fisher Please may we accept your earlier offer to show us around the city?
Chips Mmm, well, like I'm a busy cat; I may have other—engagements...
Mr Wheeler Please?
Chips (*after a pause*) OK. Come on. (*He leads them back to the "kerb"*) Rule number one in the city coming up—crossing roads—stand, wait—then...

SONG 5: Use Your Eyes And Ears

(*Singing*) Use your eyes and ears
Before you use your feet
Look and listen
Before you cross the street
Double check and when you're satisfied
Walk don't run
To the other side.
(*Speaking*) OK? Do you think you can remember that?
Mr Fisher Er... (*Singing unaccompanied*)
Use your ears and feet
Mr Wheeler Before you blow your nose...
Chips No!
Mr Fisher Oh dear.
Mr Wheeler You'd better teach us again, Chips, please.
Chips OK. (*Idea, taking in the audience*) We'll *all* teach you. (*To the audience*) Will you help the Gnomes and sing it with me?
Audience Yes.
Chips You will?
Audience Yes.
Chips Great.

At this point Chips teaches the song to the audience. A songsheet could be used, or Chips could chalk the words on the wall, but in the original production the audience picked up the song with ease, simply learning it from Chips, with actions to suit the words. The routine used is as follows

Right. Everybody, stand up.

The House Lights come up as the audience is encouraged to stand

Now, we're going to learn it in three chunks. I'll sing it first, and then you all sing it after me. First chunk coming up, after three. One, two, three...
(*Singing unaccompanied*)
Use your eyes and ears
Before you use your feet
(*Speaking*) Ready? One, two, three...

Act 1, Scene 2

Chips } Use your eyes and ears
Audience } Before you use your feet
Chips Very good. Don't forget the actions. Once more. One, two, three ...
Chips } Use your eyes and ears
Audience } Before you use your feet
Chips Next bit.
  (*Singing*)   Look and listen
                 Before you cross the street
  (*Speaking*) Ready?
Chips } Look and listen
Audience } Before you cross the street
Chips Very good. Just once more.
Chips } Look and listen
Audience } Before you cross the street
Chips Last bit.
  (*Singing*)   Double check and when you're satisfied
                 Walk don't run
                 To the other side.
  (*Speaking*) Ready?
Chips } Double check and when you're satisfied
Audience } Walk don't run
                 To the other side.
Chips Just one more try.
Chips } Double check and when you're satisfied
Audience } Walk don't run
                 To the other side.
Chips Right. Now let's put it all together. After three. One, two, three ...

The Gnomes join in the words and actions, Baby Duck does the actions

All   Use your eyes and ears
             Before you use your feet
             Look and listen
             Before you cross the street
             Double check and when you're satisfied
             Walk don't run
             To the other side.
Chips Great! *They*'ve got it. How about you, Mr Fisher, Mr Wheeler?
Mr Fisher Well, nearly, I think ...
Mr Wheeler Just once more, Chips, and we'll know it.
Chips OK. Everybody. One, two, three
All   Use your eyes and ears
             Before you use your feet
             Look and listen
             Before you cross the street
             Double check and when you're satisfied
             Walk don't run
             To the other side.
Mr Fisher I think I've got it! (*To the audience*) Thank you, everybody.

Mr Wheeler So have I. (*To the audience*) Thank you.
Chips Terrific! Thanks, everyone. You can sit down now.

The House Lights fade

Mr Wheeler Can we cross now, Chips?
Chips OK. This time it's for real!

This time they sing the song, following each action on the "real" road

Mr Fisher ⎫ Use your eyes and ears
Mr Wheeler ⎬ Before you use your feet
Chips ⎭ Look and listen
             Before you cross the street

Pause as they look and listen. No sound or light

             Double check

Another pause as they look and listen

             And when you're satisfied

They nod to each other

             Walk don't run
             To the other side.

Music continues as happily and confidently they "cross the road"

The Lights fade to a Black-out

Scene 3

The Adventure Playground

(*If at the end of the previous scene, the characters have crossed the road by walking "out front"—towards the audience—into a Black-out, it is suggested they stay on stage for the scene change, turn round, backs to the audience, and, when the Lights come up, walk into the scene*)

Downstage we see a section of the wire-netting fence surrounding the playground. Also part of the entrance gate, which is closed, but under which there is just enough room for the characters to crawl. (In one production, a corner of the wire netting was loose, thus enabling the characters to creep in that way.) Signs and notices are visible in this area—"ADVENTURE PLAYGROUND" above the entrance; "KEEP OUT", "BEWARE OF THE GUARD DOG", "TRESPASSERS WILL BE PROSECUTED" on the gate or fence. A red burglar alarm system is attached to the fence, with "BURGLAR ALARM" written on it

Upstage of the fence and gate section is a corner of the playground itself. It has a large rubber tyre (from a bus or lorry?) suspended like a trapeze from the flies. (This could be a simple swing.) Also a tube of pipe lying horizontally on the ground. This should be about five feet long, with enough room for the characters to crawl through it, like a tunnel. Finally, we can see a dog kennel, marked "SECURIDOG". Its occupant is not visible. A food bowl is positioned just outside; it is marked "Doggy Dins"

Act 1, Scene 3   21

The Adventure Playground should be as colourful as possible. It is still evening—atmospheric "darkness". Street-lamp-type lighting making things visible in shafts of light. In fact, in this scene, we need to see the action clearly

The Gnomes, Baby Duck and Chips arrive outside the Adventure Playground

Chips OK, so now we've crossed the road, like where do we go from here?
Mr Wheeler Well, Chips, our dream is to discover what the Big Ones call an island.
Mr Fisher Sun and sea and fish.

Baby Duck quacks

Chips An island. No problem. Follow me.

He leads them a step or two. Then suddenly he stops dead. Perhaps the others concertina into him. Chips sniffs—picking up a scent

Mr Wheeler What is it?

Chips moves fitfully, sniffing the air

Chips Can't you sniff it?
Mr Wheeler Sniff it? Sniff what?
Chips A whiff.
Mr Fisher Sniff a whiff? Sniff a whiff of what?
Chips Sniff a whiff of yummy, scrummy—Doggy Dins!
Mr Wheeler Doggy Dins?
Chips Mm. Meaty, mouthwatering, magnificent Doggy Dins! One of my favourite-flavoured foods.
Mr Fisher Where?
Chips (*after a big sniff*) There. Over there. (*He turns, sees the kennel and bowl, and reacts angrily*) Aaaaah! Typical. Typical. (*He stomps away*)

The others follow

Mr Fisher Isn't the whiff you sniffed Doggy Dins after all?
Chips Of course it's Doggy Dins. But look whose Doggy Dins it is.

They turn

   Securidog's!

Dramatic chord

Mr Wheeler Securidog's?
Chips Isn't that just my luck? Starving. Get a sniff. Securidog's Doggy Dins.
Mr Fisher I'm sorry, I don't get it.
Chips *You* don't get it! *I* don't get it. I don't get any Doggy Dins. Look. Behind this fence is the Adventure Playground. Right?
Mr Wheeler Er—right.
Mr Fisher Sorry, but what's an Adventure Playground?
Chips What's an Adventure Playground? Don't you Gnomes know nothing? An Adventure Playground is *ground* where children *play* and have *adventures*. Right!

Mr Fisher Ah. Right.
Chips At night it's locked up, right?
Mr Fisher } Right.
Mr Wheeler }

Baby Duck quacks at the same time

Chips Securidog guards it, right?
Mr Fisher } Right.
Mr Wheeler }

Baby Duck quacks with them

Chips Securidog loves Doggy Dins and hates cats, right?
Mr Fisher } Right.
Mr Wheeler }

Baby Duck quacks with them

Chips So no Doggy Dins for poor old Chips, right?
Mr Fisher } (*together*) Right.
Mr Wheeler }

Baby Duck quacks with them

Mr Wheeler Wrong. You've helped us, so we'll help you. Or try to.
Chips Help me?
Mr Wheeler We'll crawl under here with my wheelbarrow—(*he indicates the space under the gate*)—and ask Securidog, very politely, if he can spare some of his Doggy Dins for a deserving cause. You.
Mr Fisher But, Mr Wheeler, is it safe?
Chips Like Securidog is pretty fierce.

Baby Duck starts quacking excitedly. He has spotted the notices hanging on the fence and gate

Mr Fisher Mm? What?

Baby Duck quacks, pointing at the signs

What are they? Chips?
Chips Signs. With writing on. Can anyone read them? (*He encourages the audience to read them out*)
Audience "Burglar Alarm"; "Keep Out"; "Beware of the Guard Dog"; "Trespassers Will Be Prosecuted".
Mr Fisher "Burglar Alarm"; "Keep Out"; "Beware of the Guard Dog"; "Trespassers Will Be Prosecuted"? Mr Wheeler, we can't possibly risk going in there—just to get some Doggy Dins.
Mr Wheeler But Chips *needs* it ... What's this place called again?
Chips An Adventure Playground.
Mr Wheeler Well, this is a real adventure playground adventure!
Chips OK, *I'll* come.
Mr Wheeler Mr Fisher?

Silence. Then ...

Act 1, Scene 3

SONG 6: **A Real Adventure Playground Adventure**

During the song, Baby Duck tends to side with Mr Fisher, who gets in quite a state; they both point out the signs as Mr Fisher mentions them

(*Singing*)	Let's go in
Mr Fisher	It says "Keep Out"
Chips	But think of all that food
Mr Fisher	'Beware of the Guard Dog"
Mr Wheeler	He won't bite if we're not rude
Mr Fisher	"Burglar Alarm"
Mr Wheeler } Chips	Mr Fisher, please keep calm!
Mr Fisher	"Trespassers Will Be Prosecuted"
Mr Wheeler } Chips	We're not doing any harm.
	It's a real adventure playground aventure Don't you see?
Mr Fisher	But I really don't think we ought
Mr Wheeler	It's a quest to help a friend
Chips	Who happens to be me
Mr Fisher	But what happens if we all get caught?
Chips	Oh come on!
Mr Fisher	It says "Keep Out"
Mr Wheeler	Well, you can stay out here
Mr Fisher	"Beware of the Guard Dog"
Chips	We'll be careful, never fear
Mr Fisher	"Burglar alarm"
Chips } Mr Wheeler	If we set it off we run
Mr Fisher	"Trespassers Will Be Prosecuted"
Chips } Mr Wheeler	We're not hurting anyone.
	It's a real adventure playground adventure
Mr Fisher	Yes, I know But I really do think it's wrong I'll stay here with Baby Duck Good luck
Chips } Mr Wheeler	Right, off we go Now don't worry 'cos we won't be long.

Mr Fisher and Baby Duck remain behind by the fence as gingerly Mr Wheeler and Chips crawl under the gate, and inside. The lighting focuses inside the Adventure Playground. Music echoes the tension

During the following action Mr Fisher unobtrusively sits, looking into the Playground, and eventually goes to sleep. Baby Duck stays with him

Mr Wheeler and Chips approach the kennel. Mr Wheeler motions Chips to hide behind the kennel. Mr Wheeler knocks on the kennel. No reaction. He knocks again. No reaction. He goes to knock again. As he does so, Securidog pops out, taking him by surprise

Securidog Whadja name and whadja game?
Mr Wheeler I beg your pardon?
Securidog Whadja name and whadja game? Whadja doing here?
Mr Wheeler I ...
Securidog I'll tell you whadja doing here. You're trespassing, and trespassers will be prosecuted so prosecuted you will be. Forthwith, straightway and without further ado. Whadja name? (*He takes out a notebook and pencil*)
Mr Wheeler Listen ...
Securidog I don't listen. My ears are trained not to listen.
Mr Wheeler But look ...
Securidog I don't look. My eyes are trained not to look.
Mr Wheeler You don't listen. You don't look. That's a bit stupid, don't you think?
Securidog I don't think. My brain is trained not to think.
Mr Wheeler You're not trained to do anything, by the sound of it.
Securidog Oh yes I am. I am a trained trapper of trespassers. So there.
Mr Wheeler Well, I'm not a trespasser. I've come to ask you a question. Are you trained to answer questions?
Securidog Is it an easy question or a hard question?
Mr Wheeler Easy.
Securidog All right, then, I'll have a go. (*He concentrates*)
Mr Wheeler It's to do with your Doggy Dins. (*He points to the bowl*)
Securidog Yes?
Mr Wheeler I have a friend, a cat, who is extremely hungry.
Securidog Yes?
Mr Wheeler Who is very partial to Doggy Dins.
Securidog Yes?
Mr Wheeler The question is, could you spare some?
Securidog Yes.
Mr Wheeler Oh thank you, I'll just ... (*He goes to load some on his wheelbarrow*)
Securidog Stop! I said yes, I *could* spare some; I didn't say I was *going* to spare some. And I'm not. For a cat! I hate cats. And I hate friends of cats. So clear off before ...
Mr Wheeler But he's starving ...
Securidog Good. I'm glad. Clear off ...
Mr Wheeler Please ...
Securidog Or I'll throw you against the fence and make the alarm bell ring and then the Big Ones'll come and sort you out. Clear off. (*He stomps back inside his kennel*)

Music. Mr Wheeler takes his wheelbarrow and turns to go. He sees Chips, downcast, appear from behind the kennel. He stops. Mr Wheeler looks at the

Act 1, Scene 3

bowl of food, back to Chips, then to the kennel—there is no sign of Securidog. Mr Wheeler turns to the audience

Mr Wheeler (*in a stage whisper*) Shall I take some?
Audience (*encouraged not to shout, but whisper back*) Yes.
Mr Wheeler (*in a whisper*) Chips.

He beckons Chips over, and quickly mimes taking some food. Very gingerly Mr Wheeler takes a chunk of dog food, and passes it to Chips who loads it into the wheelbarrow. And another chunk. And another. Suddenly Securidog bursts out of the kennel. Mr Wheeler and Chips naturally scatter to avoid capture or rough handling

Securidog Right. You asked for it and you're going to get it. (*Seeing Chips*) And you, you mangy moggy. Thieves will be prosecuted, and prosecuted you will be. Forthwith, straightway and without further ado.

Mr Wheeler and his wheelbarrow back away, then head gingerly for the gate. Chips leaps into the suspended tyre and crouches, swinging. Securidog has come out further than we have seen him before. We now see he is tethered to the kennel and cannot chase the others any further

(*Seeing and grabbing the wheelbarrow*) Right. For a start I'm confiscating this. This will be Exhibit A.

Mr Wheeler Not my wheelbarrow, please.
Securidog It contains stolen property. Kidnapped Doggy Dins. Exhibit B. Now, you two, come here. You'll be Exhibits C and—and—four.
Chips Hey. Look, Mr Wheeler. He's tied to the kennel. He can't chase us, let alone catch us. (*Taunting*) Cooee, Securidog, come and catch me! Cooee! (*He leans down provocatively from the tyre*)
Securidog You cheeky cat, you'll regret that ... (*He charges, but can't get far enough, because his tether won't stretch any more. He growls with frustration*)
Chips Oh, he's cross. Look. My, my. Like he's at the end of his tether! (*He laughs*)
Mr Wheeler (*approaching*) Now, Chips. Don't tease the poor fellow. After all, it can't be much fun being tied up.
Securidog It's not. I hate it.
Mr Wheeler The Big Ones, I bet?
Securidog What?
Mr Wheeler I bet it was the Big Ones tied you up?
Securidog Yes. Said I might not do my job if I wasn't tied up. Said I might run away.
Mr Wheeler Might you?
Securidog Maybe.
Mr Wheeler (*deliberately buttering him up*) You don't enjoy being nasty to people, do you?
Securidog I'm only doing my job.
Mr Wheeler You're quite friendly really, aren't you (*He strokes him*)
Securidog I *would* be, but I haven't got any friends. Mm, that's nice!

Mr Wheeler Be my friend.
Securidog Mm. That's lovely. How?
Mr Wheeler Give me back my wheelbarrow.
Securidog What? (*Snapping out of his trance*) You're just trying to get round me, aren't you? All that stroking. If I give you back your wheelbarrow I'll never see you again. Fine friend you'd be.
Mr Wheeler But I need my wheelbarrow. If I go home without it, the Big Ones where I live will notice it's gone.
Securidog Oh, that's all right, then.
Mr Wheeler I beg your pardon?
Securidog Because you're not going home. You're Exhibit C.
Mr Wheeler But you're forgetting. You can't stop me going home.
Securidog Why not?
Mr Wheeler Because you're tied to your kennel.

Pause. This sinks in

Securidog Tell you what.
Mr Wheeler What?
Securidog I'll give you back your wheelbarrow...
Mr Wheeler Thank you.
Securidog And a few chunks of Doggy Dins...
Mr Wheeler Oh, thank you.

He moves forward. But Securidog still holds the wheelbarrow

Securidog Wait for it! If...
Mr Wheeler Yes?
Securidog And only if...
Mr Wheeler What?
Securidog You untie me.
Mr Wheeler Ah... I untie you?
Securidog That's fair. Whadja say? (*He smiles innocently*)
Mr Wheeler Well...
Chips (*who has been listening from the tyre*) Don't trust him, Mr Wheeler. It's a trick.
Mr Wheeler But I must get my wheelbarrow back.
Securidog Untie me and it's yours.
Chips He'll doublecross you. He's just said he might run away.
Mr Wheeler But you need some Doggy Dins.
Chips But if we let him go I might not be around long enough to eat them.
Mr Wheeler Oh dear... (*Idea—he turns to the audience*) What do *you* think we should do? Untie him? Yes? No?

If the majority shout "Yes", Mr Wheeler says "All right". If the majority shout "No", he says "But I really think I must." Tension music as he approaches Securidog, who smiles, looking as good as gold. Mr Wheeler unties his tether and puts the rope down by the kennel. Securidog politely hands over the wheelbarrow. He puts some chunks of Doggy Dins in it. Mr Wheeler wheels it away towards Chips, who leaps down to meet it. Just as we think the exchange has gone well...

Act 1, Scene 3   27

Securidog Ha, ha, ha. I'm free. I'm free. I'll get you. I'll get you!

He charges at the retreating pair, who react horrified. Exciting music echoes the ensuing chase sequence. Chips dashes to the tyre again. Securidog makes for Mr Wheeler. The wheelbarrow is between them. They play a cat and mouse game around it—both side-stepping left, right, then left again. Then Securidog chases Mr Wheeler round the barrow. Once. Twice. On the third round, Securidog waits, and trips up Mr Wheeler as he comes round. Mr Wheeler falls on the ground. Securidog grabs the barrow, and wheels it back towards the kennel, passing Chips in the tyre, who lashes out at him, but can't reach. Securidog wheels the barrow into his kennel. Chips jumps down and goes to look at the prostrate Mr Wheeler. Securidog emerges from the kennel, having left the barrow inside. He sees Chips, facing away from him, and advances

The audience will probably shout a warning

Chips turns in the nick of time, and runs to the tyre. Securidog follows. A short chase round the tyre, then Chips nimbly leaps through it. Securidog tries to follow, but gets stuck half-way through. Chips gives him a couple of kicks up the backside. If possible Chips climbs on to the top of the tyre, above Securidog. Securidog suddenly spots Mr Wheeler getting up and heading for the kennel to retrieve his barrow. He extricates himself from the tyre, giving it a good swing, making Chips hang on grimly. Securidog cuts off Mr Wheeler's progress to the kennel. He makes a grab for him, but Mr Wheeler ducks and nimbly darts through Securidog's legs, and runs towards the pipe. Mr Wheeler enters the pipe. Securidog follows him through and "flushes" him out of the other end. Mr Wheeler runs round and into the pipe again. Securidog follows. Another flushing

But by now, Baby Duck, outside the playground, has been watching in alarm, and woken Mr Fisher, who, seeing his chance, leaving his fishing-rod behind, crawls under the gate. Just as Mr Wheeler enters the pipe a third time. Mr Fisher calls out. The Music stops momentarily so that we can hear him

Mr Fisher Coo-ee!

Securidog turns and sees Mr Fisher. He is confused, because the Gnomes look so similar. He looks back at the pipe, scratching his head

Securidog Eh? Howdja get over there?

He makes towards Mr Fisher, who runs between his legs, inside the pipe. Securidog leaps on top of the pipe, hoping to grab Mr Fisher as he comes out. Suddenly Mr Wheeler pops his head out of the other end

Mr Wheeler Coo-ee!

Securidog stops in his tracks—how did the gnome get through the pipe so quickly? He dashes to Mr Wheeler's end. Mr Wheeler pops back in. Simultaneously Mr Fisher pops out again at his end

Mr Fisher Coo-ee!

Securidog turns back, totally mystified. He starts back to Mr Fisher's end. Simultaneously, Mr Fisher disappears and Mr Wheeler pops his head out

Mr Wheeler Coo-ee!

Securidog stands C on the pipe in confusion. He looks back to Mr Fisher's end. Two legs appear. Securidog now sees what appears to be a very long gnome— Mr Wheeler's head and Mr Fisher's legs poking out

Securidog (*Facing front*) Aaaaaaaaaaah!

Now the Gnomes both turn round—i.e. Mr Fisher's head and Mr Wheeler's legs are visible. Securidog looks again. He reacts

(*Facing front*) Aaaaaaaaaaah!

Now Mr Wheeler stays as he is and Mr Fisher changes position—so four legs poke out. Securidog looks again. He reacts

(*Facing front*) Aaaaaaaaaaah!

The final coup! Both Gnomes change positions—so two heads pop out. Securidog rubs his eyes in disbelief, then turns again. He reacts

Aaaaaaaaaaaaaaaaaaah!

Chips sees his chance. He jumps down from the tyre, and dashes into the kennel to retrieve Mr Wheeler's barrow. Securidog sees him and follows, into the kennel. Terrible sounds of a fight emerge from inside the kennel. Eventually Chips dashes out—with the barrow—and hides—maybe behind the pipe. The Gnomes hide inside the pipe. Securidog emerges, raging from the kennel. He can see nothing

Then, suddenly, outside the fence, Baby Duck starts strutting up and down. Securidog registers this with surprise. Baby Duck looks at him through the fence. He looks at Baby Duck. Securidog barks ferociously. Baby Duck doesn't move, but quacks. Securidog jumps back, terrified. He barks again; Baby Duck quacks; he jumps back again. Then Securidog charges like a bull towards Baby Duck. He crashes into the wire fence. Baby Duck retreats into the shadows

Immediately all hell is let loose. First the loud clanging of the burglar alarm, then police sirens, flashing blue lights. A car arrives. Doors slam. Voices boom from above

Voice 1 Who's there? What's going on?
Voice 2 Come on out, whoever you are.

A Searchlight (a police torch) swings around and comes to rest on Securidog cowering by the fence

Voice 1 Hey look, it's only Securidog. He's escaped. Set the alarm off.
Voice 2 Get back in your kennel, you stupid animal.
Voice 1 Wasting our time.

Securidog, tail between his legs as it were, meekly returns to his kennel, looking at the Big Ones above

Voice 2 And you can stay in there till the morning. We don't want any more false alarms.

Act 1, Scene 3

Securidog gets in the kennel.

The searchlight goes out. The car doors slam and the car drives off. The lighting returns to normal

The Gnomes emerge from the pipe, and Chips plus barrow. Baby Duck comes to meet them. They all shake hands, then start going under the gate. Chips stops, turns back, goes towards the kennel, and takes a few more chunks of dog-food from the bowl and returns to the others, outside the gate. Mr Wheeler takes back his barrow. Chips takes a chunk of dog food and starts to eat it

Chips Thank you Gnomes, thank you, Baby Duck. Maybe holidays aren't so bad after all! Now ...

SONG 6: **Holiday Island** (Reprise)

(*Singing*)	Let's find your holiday island
Mr Wheeler } **Mr Fisher** }	Our holiday do or die land
All	Where there's nothing to do
	But enjoy doing nothing
	Where there's nothing to do
	But have fun
	Let's find our holiday yours and my land
	Pie in the sky land
	Do or die land
	Island in the sun.

They start to exit, perhaps through the auditorium. Baby Duck collects Mr Fisher's fishing-rod for him

     Let's find our holiday island
     Yours and my land
     Pie in the sky land
     Do or die land
     Island in the sun.

     (*Optional repeat*)
     Let's find our holiday island
     Yours and my land
     Pie in the sky land
     Do or die land
     Island in the sun.

They exit

CURTAIN

ACT 2

Scene 1

The Street

We see the edge of the kerb of a pavement; the pavement is a rostrum, behind which there could be a backing of doors, shopfronts or a wall. There is a drain at road level, with the usual grating effect. Immediately in front of the kerb, there is a patch of wet tar, with a notice to inform us of the fact, surrounded by a few red and white cones and maybe a warning lantern

To the other side, there is a road works section, with a barrier, a sign and some more red and white cones

Wacker, the pneumatic bouncer, is standing or lying horizontally on the pavement behind the tar. He remains lifeless until started up, and should not be lit too visibly yet

It is still night-time, but street lighting effects should make the pavement and drain side of the stage clearly, though atmospherically, visible. The road works side should be fairly dark. Perhaps we hear a clock chime two a.m.

    Music as Chips enters energetically, turns and looks off, then beckons. He jumps off the pavement, between the drain and the road works

    Baby Duck enters

    Chips helps him down from the pavement, then exits

Baby Duck starts to exit, then sees the wet tar. He spots the "WET TAR" notice. He scratches his head, unable to read the sign. He looks at the audience and quacks a request for them to read the sign. Hopefully they read out "Wet Tar". Baby Duck goes to the tar and starts to dip his foot in, looking at the audience as if to say "Shall I?" The audience should warn him not to. He repeats this

    Chips dashes on and pulls Baby Duck away from the tar

Chips Hey, duck. Come away. Like that's wet tar.

Baby Duck quacks that he knows that—the audience told him. He returns to the tar and starts to put his foot in it. Chips grabs him again

    NO! It's what the Big Ones use to mend the road. It's very sticky. If you tread in it you might never get out.

Baby Duck quacks, alarmed

Act 2, Scene 1

SONG 7: **Stuck Duck**

(*Singing*) Don't put
Your foot
In the muck, Duck
This black tacky
Tarmacky
Muck, Duck
If you put
Your foot
In the muck, Duck
You can bet
Your luck
You'll get
Stuck, Duck

It's icky and ucky
As ucky as can be
So sticky and yucky
You won't get free

Suddenly Baby Duck runs down. Chips rewinds him. Baby Duck cheekily comes to life again and heads for the tar. Chips restrains him

Don't put
Your foot
In the muck, Duck
This black tacky
Tarmacky
Muck, Duck
If you put
Your foot
In the muck, Duck
You can bet
Your luck
Lor' luv a duck
You can bet
Your luck
You'll get
Stuck, Duck

(*Speaking*) Right?

Baby Duck quacks

We hear Mr Fisher groan off-stage

Chips look off. He beckons

(*Calling*) Come on, you two, keep up.

Mr Fisher enters, carrying his fishing-rod. He is tired

Mr Fisher Ohhh. Keep up, he says; I can't even keep awake.

Chips helps him down from the pavement

Chips Well, you didn't expect your holiday island to be round the next corner, did you?

Mr Fisher yawns and stops, virtually nodding off on the spot

Come on, Mr Wheeler.

Mr Wheeler enters, pushing his wheelbarrow. He, too, is exhausted.

Chips gives him a hand

Mr Wheeler How much further, Chips? My legs are dropping off.

Without noticing at first, he pushes the barrow into Mr Fisher, who drops backwards down into it, and immediately snores loudly

Chips Mr Fisher's dropped off already.

Baby Duck tries to wake Mr Fisher. He quacks. No reaction. Mr Wheeler tries

Mr Wheeler Mr Fisher.

No reaction

Mr Fisher.

Chips (*pulling on the fishing-line*) Oi!

Mr Fisher (*springing into action with his rod*) A bite! A bite! Heave! Heave! Come on my beauty! (*Realizing*) Oh, Chips, it's you.

Mr Wheeler It's all right, Mr Fisher. We're all here.

Mr Fisher Where? The island?

Chips Not much further, Mr Fisher. Come on ... (*Helping him up*) You can't throw in the towel now.

Mr Fisher I haven't the strength to throw in a handkerchief.

Mr Wheeler Chips, I think we all need a rest.

Baby Duck quacks indignantly, waddling vigorously

Chips *He* doesn't. I've just wound him up.

Mr Wheeler Well, Mr Fisher and I do. We're just not used to all this energetic exercise.

Chips OK. We'll have a quick kip.

Mr Fisher Oh, thank goodness.

Mr Wheeler Thank you.

They start to settle down to sleep

Fluffy Duck, you too.

Baby Duck quacks and shakes his head

You don't want a sleep?

Baby Duck quacks "No"

Chips Like I told you. I just wound him up.

Mr Wheeler Oh dear. That means he's full of beans; he'll never sleep. (*To Baby Duck*) Well, stay here,then. Don't wander off. Exploring.

Act 2, Scene 1

Baby Duck quacks, a little defiantly

Mr Fisher Don't worry, Mr Wheeler. (*Yawning*) He can look after himself. (*He settles to sleep*)
Mr Wheeler But he's only a baby duck.
Chips Listen, I'll stay awake and make sure he doesn't get into danger.
Mr Wheeler Would you? Thank you. I'd hate anything to happen to him.
Chips No problem. (*He yawns*) You have a kip, and I'll stay awake. (*He yawns again*)
Mr Wheeler (*not sure*) Mm. Good-night.
Chips Night.
Mr Wheeler Good-night, Mr Fisher.

Mr Fisher snores loudly

Good-night, Fluffy Duck.

Baby Duck quacks. Mr Wheeler goes to sleep. Chips remains awake

Music — sleepy music

Chips yawns and nods off to sleep. Straight-away he snaps out of it

Chips Brrrrrr (*a keeping-awake noise*). Must keep awake.

Music

Chips yawns and nods off again. Straightaway he snaps out of it

Brrrrr. Must keep awake. (*He perhaps does a quick exercise, or hits himself*)

Music. Chips nods off, fast asleep

After a pause, Baby Duck stirs, gets up, and waddles off. The audience may well shout out a warning, but Baby Duck tries to keep them quiet, taking them into his confidence as he explores. Whatever happens he goes over to the road works side, avoids the tar and investigates the road works sign, cones, etc. Then he wanders round behind. If necessary he climbs up on to the pavement rostrum. He finds the inert Wacker and quacks, fascinated. He looks along the length of it, then prods it. Seeing a button or lever, he presses it

Wacker roars into life. A sound effect of a pneumatic engine starting up could be used. Wacker bounces happily, though menacingly, into full view. The startled Baby Duck gets out of vision of Wacker, who bounces about singing

SONG 8: I'm Wacker!

Wacker Whack, whack,
Whacketty whack.
Whack, whack,
Whacketty whack.

I'm Wacker
I'm Wacker

And I pack a
Punch
Whacking the tar
With a crack and a
Crunch
I jump
And I bump
With a stamp and a pat
Smacking, attacking it
Whacking it
Flat.

Whack,
Whacketty whack,
Whack, whack,
Whacketty whack.

I whack here
I whack there
I whack any old where
I'm a wacker of no fixed abode
Nothing can stop
My hoppity hop
Unless you want whacking get out of me road.

I'm Wacker
I'm Wacker
And I pack a
Punch
Whacking away
With a crack and a
Crunch
I jump
And I bump
With a stamp and a pat
Smacking, attacking it
Whacking it
Flat.

Whack,
Whacketty whack.
Whack, whack,
Whacketty whack!

Baby Duck, intrigued emerges from the shadows to introduce himself. He quacks a greeting. Wacker is at first uncertain how to react, but then starts to show aggression

Act 2, Scene 1　　　　　　　　　　　　　　　　　　　　　　　　　　35

(*Speaking*) Whack you flat! Whack you flat! Whack you flat!

Music as he bounces after Baby Duck, chasing him along the pavement and back again. Baby Duck goes to jump off the pavement—into the wet tar area—but stops, just in time, and manages to jump safely avoiding the tar. But at this moment his clockwork starts to run down. He is paralysed—in an ideal place for Wacker to jump down on him

Ha ha! Whack you flat! Whack you flat!

Wacker prepares to jump. His engine revs up to a frightening crescendo. The audience will probably have been shouting. In any event, the Gnomes wake up, size up the situation, and dash to the rescue. They pull Baby Duck clear in the nick of time. Wacker jumps down, landing painfully on the road

Ow! (*He rubs his wacking foot*)

Meanwhile, Mr Wheeler shelters Baby Duck

Mr Fisher We should never have gone to sleep, Mr Wheeler.
Mr Wheeler Chips said he'd stay awake.

No reaction. Mr Wheeler manages to give Baby Duck two winds—ratchet noises

Mr Fisher (*dashing to Chips*) Chips!
Wacker (*moaning*) Ow!

Mr Wheeler leaves Baby Duck, and he and Mr Fisher go over to Wacker

Mr Wheeler What do you think you're doing?
Wacker I'm rubbing my whacking plate, aren't I?
Mr Wheeler I beg your pardon?
Wacker Rubbing my whacking plate. I think I've sprained a sprocket.
Mr Fisher What does that mean?
Wacker It means my whacking days may be limited. And a wacker that can't whack is worse than worthless. I'll be a whackless wacker! (*He bursts into tears*)
Mr Fisher Now, now. Don't get in a state.
Wacker I'm sorry. I'm not usually like this. I'm a happy wacker, really. A bouncy wacker. (*He tries a bounce*) Ow.
Mr Wheeler Calm down. Stand up straight.
Wacker (*doing so*) Ow.
Mr Wheeler Take his other side, Mr Fisher.

They support him

Just stand still for a while.
Wacker I can't stand still. When I get turned on, I have to whack. (*He bounces a little*)
Mr Fisher Why?
Wacker Because I'm a wacker. I was born to whack. Whacking's my whole life.
Mr Wheeler What do you whack?

Wacker Anything. Everything. Tar on roads mostly. But given the chance I'll whack anything. Everything (*He tries a few bounces*) Hey, that feels better. Thank you.
Mr Wheeler Don't mention it.
Wacker (*bouncing, testing himself*) I'm Wacker, I'm Wacker, and I pack a punch...

His bounces are now taking the Gnomes up in the air with him. They react with little "Ohs"

    Whack! Whack! Whack!

He bounces around with the Gnomes hanging on

Mr Fisher Whoa! Whoa! I'm feeling giddy!
Wacker Whack! Whack! Whack!
Mr Wheeler Let go of him, Mr Fisher.

They both let go. They fall to the ground

    Are you feeling better?
Wacker (*in rhythm*) Whack! Whack! I'm feeling fine! Thank you, you've been very kind! Whack! Whack! (*His bounces are getting bigger and wilder. He gets very near the Gnomes*)

Mr Fisher Look out! You nearly whacked us!
Wacker Sorry. I can't help it. It's my life! Whack you flat! Whack you flat! (*Back to normal, he approaches the Gnomes again*)

Tension music

Mr Wheeler Look out, Mr Fisher!
Wacker Whack you flat! Whack you flat!

The Gnomes struggle up and bump into each other trying to escape. Wacker chases them round, then up on to the pavement

    Whack you flat! Whack you flat!

The only place the Gnomes can jump down to is the wet tar area

    Into the tar! Into the tar!
Mr Fisher No, no!
Mr Wheeler Help, help!

They land in the tar. Their feet make contact, and they struggle to pull them out. The sticky mess of the tar makes this difficult

Wacker Here I come! Whack you flat! (*He prepares to jump*)
Mr Wheeler You'll sprain your whacking plate! Stop!
Wacker I can't! I'm born to whack, whack you flat!
Mr Fisher But we helped you! You can't whack *us*!
Wacker I'm sorry. Nothing personal. It's only Wacker nature. Whack you flat! (*His engine revs up to a frightening crescendo*)
Mr Fisher Help! Help!

Act 2, Scene 1

Baby Duck, who has been resting since being rescued, suddenly notices what is going on and, quacking, wakes up Chips, pointing out the plight of the Gnomes. He pushes Chips over to the Gnomes; then his clockwork starts to run down. This is hardly noticeable, because there is so much action going on elsewhere, but this helps later on. Baby Duck stops, by the drain, immobile, facing front, or lying on his side

Chips, having sized up the situation, springs to the rescue. He leaps on to the pavement and turns off Wacker's switch or lever. Wacker judders to a standstill, trying to turn himself on again

Wacker Whack ... you ... flat! ... I'll ... get ... you! ... Whack ... you ... flat! ... Whack ... (*He is still*)

Chips struggles to pull the Gnomes free of the tar

Mr Fisher You said you'd stay awake.
Chips Sorry, man. I was whacked.
Mr Fisher *You* were whacked. We nearly got whacked to smithereens.
Mr Wheeler Yes. Well, there's no time for arguments.

Chips pulls them free

Thank you, Chips. Now, please get us out of here before Wacker attacks again.
Chips It's OK. He's off now.
Mr Wheeler Well, I think *we* should be off now too. This was meant to be a dream holiday, not a nightmare holiday.

The Gnomes retrieve their wheelbarrow and fishing-rod

Come on, Fluffy Duck. Time to go.

Baby Duck utters a plaintive quack. All turn. He quacks again. Worried, they go to him

Mr Fisher (*seeing Baby Duck motionless*) I think he's gone to sleep.
Chips He looks a bit off colour to me.

No reaction

Mr Wheeler No, no. He's run down.
Mr Fisher So am I. I've never felt so run down in my life.
Mr Wheeler No, no, Mr Fisher. His clockwork's run down. Help me stand him up.

They stand Baby Duck up, and turn him round. Mr Wheeler goes to wind his key. The key has vanished

Mr Wheeler (*suddenly realizing, after winding an imaginary key for a moment*) Where's it gone?
Mr Fisher Where's what gone?
Mr Wheeler His key. It's disappeared. Chips, where's his key?
Chips Search me.

Mr Wheeler We must search everywhere. Without his key, Fluffy Duck will never work again.

They look around on the ground. The audience may shout out "Down the drain". In any event ...

Chips *(after a pause)* I've got it!
Mr Wheeler Thank goodness. Give it here.
Chips No—I don't mean I've got it, I mean I've got it, get it?
Mr Wheeler No.
Chips An idea. Like where was he lying?
Mr Fisher There.
Chips Right, it's fallen down there.
Mr Wheeler Where?
Chips There. The drain.
Mr Fisher Drain? What's a drain?
Chips *(showing them)* This. It's where the rainwater goes. The key must have dropped through.
Mr Wheeler There's water down there?
Chips And a key. I bet.
Mr Fisher *(pulling at the drain)* We'll never get it back from down there, Mr Wheeler.
Mr Wheeler *(idea)* Yes, we will. That is to say, *you* will, Mr Fisher.
Mr Fisher I will?
Mr Wheeler This is your moment, Mr Fisher. Fetch your fishing-rod!
Mr Fisher My ... *(Realizing)* Of course! My fishing-rod.

Music starts as he takes his rod, sits cross-legged on the kerb, and dangles the line down the drain. The others watch eagerly

SONG 9: **Sitting Fishing**

(Singing) Sitting
Fishing
Dangling my line
Sitting
Thinking
Nothing's so fine
Sitting
Fishing
Rod in my hand
Sitting
Fishing
Nothing's so grand.

Sitting
Fishing
Hope for a bite
Sitting
Thinking

Act 2, Scene 1

> Life is all right
> Sitting
> Fishing
> That's how I find
> Perfect
> Pleasure
> Pure peace of mind.
>
> I may not be fishing for fishes
> But that doesn't matter to me
> I'm not fishing for fishes
> Or wishing for fishes
> My wish is
> To fish for a key.

As Mr Fisher sings the last verse, the others join in, singing in harmony or to "Ah"

> Sitting
> Fishing
> Dangling my line
> Sitting
> Thinking
> Nothing's so fine
> Sitting
> Fishing
> Rod in my hand
> Sitting
> Fishing
> Nothing's so grand.

(*Speaking*) A bite! A bite! Heave-ho, my beauty!

Tension music as he slowly pulls up the key. Mr Fisher is radiant. All are delighted. The music continues as Mr Wheeler takes the key off the hook, and winds up Baby Duck. Ratchet noises. Baby Duck quacks happily back into action, then bows a thank you. All cheer and applaud. Chips is standing quite near the immobile Wacker. He throws his arms wide, expressing delight, and, by mistake, his paw hits Wacker's "on" button. Wacker starts juddering into life

Wacker Aaaaaaaaaaaaaaaaaaaah!

All turn to see Wacker starting to jump

> I'm Wacker, I'm Wacker, and I pack a punch! I'll get you, I'll get you. Whack you flat! Whack you flat!

All panic and, collecting their things, start to scuttle off

> *Wacker chases Mr Fisher and Chips off stage*

Mr Wheeler and Baby Duck beat a hasty retreat and exit the other side

Mr Fisher and Chips return, breathless. Wacker is still heard in pursuit

Chips pushes Mr Fisher towards the side Mr Wheeler and Baby Duck exited

Mr Fisher exits to safety

Chips thinks quickly what to do. He indicates to the audience that his plan is to lure Wacker into the wet tar. Then he positions himself behind it

Wacker enters. He stops

(*To the audience*) Where are they?

Audience There!
Wacker Where?
Audience There!

Wacker turns and sees Chips, who makes rude faces at him

Wacker Whack you flat! Whack you flat! I'll get you! (*He jumps towards Chips, and lands in the tar. He struggles unsuccessfully to get out*)

Chips runs off, laughing and thanking the audience

Wacker makes a big effort to follow, but loses his balance and falls headlong into the wet tar. He lies there, helpless

Aaaaaaaaaaaaaaaaaaaah! I'm stuck!

The lights fade to a black-out as he squirms like a stranded whale

Scene 2

The Island

In order to cover the scene change, it is suggested that immediately after the end of Scene 1, Chips is discovered in a follow-spot, beckoning to the others to escape. He leads them off-stage — into the auditorium. Chips, Mr Fisher, Mr Wheeler (plus wheelbarrow) and Baby Duck hurry through the audience, escaping from the possibly-pursuing Wacker

Meanwhile, a front-cloth or tabs fly in to cover the scene change. This is completed by the time the characters return to the stage

The scene opens on an empty stage. Dawn

Chips and the others remain at one side of the stage, breathless, having a quick rest. Baby Duck quacks, worried, looking back in the direction from which they have come

Mr Wheeler It's all right, Fluffy Duck, I don't think Wacker's following us.
Chips Still wallowing in the tar, I reckon.
Mr Fisher Serve him right, trying to whack us.
Mr Wheeler Oh, Mr Fisher, that's unfair, he didn't *want* to whack us, but whacking's all he knows about, poor fellow.

Act 2, Scene 2

Mr Fisher Chips was right. This concrete jungle, as he calls it, isn't safe to explore on your own. Wackers, Securidogs, crossing the road...
Chips Talking of which here's another road to cross right now...
Mr Fisher Oh dear...
Chips Don't get in a sweat, Mr Fisher. Last one.
Mr Wheeler Last one? You mean...
Chips Island here we come. Over this road and you're there.

All react excitedly

Mr Fisher Jumping toadstools. What are we waiting for? (*He steps forward*)

Immediately there is the loud roar of a car passing, plus the strong beam of headlights. Chips grabs Mr Fisher back

Chips Easy, Mr Fisher, easy. You've forgotten the song, haven't you?

Mr Fisher looks uneasy

Mr Wheeler?

Mr Wheeler shakes his head

(*To the audience*) Come on, everyone, let's remind them. Everybody up!

The audience is encouraged to stand. The House Lights come up

One, two, three...

SONG 9a: **Use Your Eyes And Ears** (Reprise)

Chips ⎫ Use your eyes and ears
Audience ⎭ Before you use your feet
　　　　　　Look and listen
　　　　　　Before you cross the street
　　　　　　Double check and when you're satisfied
　　　　　　Walk don't run
　　　　　　To the other side.
Chips (*to the audience*) Thank you!

He looks at the Gnomes, who are still uncertain

Just one more time; then they'll *never* forget. One, two, three...
Chips ⎫ Use your eyes and ears
Audience ⎭ Before you use your feet
　　　　　　Look and listen
　　　　　　Before you cross the street
　　　　　　Double check and when you're satisfied
　　　　　　Walk don't run
　　　　　　To the other side.
Chips Thanks very much, everyone. You can sit down now.

The House Lights fade

(*To the Gnomes*) Mr Fisher, Mr Wheeler. You're on your own.

Mr Fisher and Mr Wheeler nervously sing
Mr Fisher ⎱ Use your eyes and ears
Mr Wheeler ⎰ Before you use your feet
　　　　　　　Look and listen
　　　　　　　Before you cross the street

Pause as they look and listen

　　　　　　　Double check

Pause as they double check

　　　　　　　And when you're satisfied
　　　　　　　Walk don't run to the other side.

Chips You've got it!

The music continues as all four "cross the road"—perhaps walking on the spot

The music builds to the entrance of the "island". A traffic island. This is hopefully on a truck, and comes to meet them. It has a flashing Belisha beacon and two bollards

All except Mr Fisher jump on when it arrives in position. Chips sits on a bollard

Mr Fisher (*disappointed*) Is this it?
Chips This is it.
Mr Fisher This is an island?
Chips Like it's the only island I know. A traffic island.
Mr Fisher I see.
Mr Wheeler Cheer up, Mr Fisher.
Mr Fisher Well, I'm sorry. I'm very grateful to Chips for bringing us here. But I must admit it's not quite what I'd expected.
Mr Wheeler How do you mean?
Mr Fisher Well, I can't really imagine the Big Ones coming *here* for their holidays. As I understand it, they go to an island to get away from all the problems of living in a city.
Chips Right on! Say no more! This traffic island's where *I* come to get away from all the problems of living in a city.
Mr Fisher Really?
Chips Of course! Here I'm safe. No traffic. No Securidogs. No Wacker. Out of sight!
Mr Wheeler He's right, Mr Fisher. Out of sight! (*He looks around*) I'm beginning to enjoy myself already.
Mr Fisher But where's the sun? Islands always have the sun.

After a pause, Baby Duck points up at the Belisha beacon

Chips That's right, Duck! This island has its own personal built-in sun. What's more, it never gets hidden behind a cloud.
Mr Wheeler He's right, Mr Fisher. And look, here's your very own seat.

He shows him a bollard. Mr Fisher clambers up

Act 2, Scene 2   43

Mr Fisher Mmm. Yes. Well, I certainly feel I could relax here.
Mr Wheeler Exactly. It's perfect, Chips. Thank you.
Chips My pleasure, Mr Wheeler.
Mr Fisher It's perfect, but for one thing ...
Chips What's that, Mr Fisher? Do my best to oblige.
Mr Fisher Water. No water. Islands are always surrounded by water.
Chips Ah. Water. (*He considers*)

There is a sudden clap of thunder. The lighting on the cyclorama darkens

Baby Duck quacks and points upwards. We hear rain beginning to fall, and perhaps see a rain effect on the cyclorama, or even projected on the island

   Here you are! *Rain*water!
Mr Fisher (*radiant*) Now it *is* perfect. Thank you, Chips!
Chips My pleasure, Mr Fisher.

SONG 9b: Holiday Island (Reprise)

Mr Fisher } Now
Mr Wheeler } We've found our holiday island
              Our holiday yours and my land
              Where there's nothing to do
              But enjoy doing nothing
              Where there's nothing to do
              But have fun
              We've found our holiday yours and my land
              Island in the sun.

They indicate the Belisha beacon. Chips joins in the song

Mr Fisher } Yes
Mr Wheeler } We've found our holiday island
Chips   Our holiday pie in the sky land
              If we're feeling too warm
              We can splash in the water

They enjoy the rain

              Then get dry in the sun's
              Golden beams
              We've found our holiday yours and my land
              Pie in the sky land
              Do or die land
              Island of our dreams.

At the end of the song, the general lighting increases. It is early morning. The rain stops

Mr Wheeler This is the best holiday we've ever had, Mr Fisher.
Mr Fisher This is the *only* holiday we've ever had, Mr Wheeler.

Baby Duck quacks, a little dejected

What? What's the matter?

Baby Duck mimes he didn't like the rain

Mr Wheeler Didn't you like the rain?
Mr Fisher We're used to rain. We're outside in all weathers.
Mr Wheeler We'd better watch you don't get all rusty. What about you, Chips? Do you mind the rain?
Chips Don't have any choice, Mr Wheeler. When you haven't got a home, a drop of rain's the least of your worries.
Mr Wheeler Of course, I'm sorry. I forgot you haven't a home.
Chips I've forgotten what it's like *having* a home.

Pause

Mr Fisher Well, talking of home, it's morning ...
Mr Wheeler You're right, Mr Fisher. Our Big Ones may well be home from Granny's soon. We'd better be on our way. Come on, Fluffy Duck.

They gather their things, rather forgetting Chips

Mr Fisher Now, cross the road; look and listen—all clear. Follow me. Home. Back to my toadstool.

The Gnomes and Baby Duck check the road and "cross". Music, as Baby Duck notices Chips still on the island. He quacks

Mr Wheeler What? (*Getting the message from Baby Duck*) Chips! (*Calling*) Chips! Aren't you coming?
Chips No hurry. No point in hurrying when you've no place to hurry to.

Pause

Mr Fisher Mr Wheeler.
Mr Wheeler Yes, Mr Fisher?
Mr Fisher Why don't we take Chips home with us?
Mr Wheeler Why not indeed? Chips. Come with us.
Chips Well ...
Mr Wheeler There's a shed in our back yard. The Big Ones never go in it except at weekends. You could sleep there.
Chips Does it have a roof?
Mr Wheeler Of course.
Chips A roof over my head again? Hey, I don't know, I'm so used to being free—like no ties.
Mr Fisher You'd still be free. Free to come and go over the wall whenever you like.
Mr Wheeler Please come. It's the least we can do to thank you for our exciting holiday.
Mr Fisher Please ...

Baby Duck quacks imploringly

Chips Well, OK, I'll try anything once!

Act 2, Scene 2   45

He jumps down. Pleased, the others start to go

And besides

They stop and turn

—you're going the wrong way!

He checks the road and crosses. The others join him

Mr Wheeler Come on then. As the Big Ones say, after a holiday, however perfect, there's nothing like going home!

The music starts

SONG 10: **Back Home**

Mr Wheeler } **Mr Fisher**	Back home To our back yard Back home It's time to go Back home Where we belong Back home To the world we know
Mr Wheeler	Back to the dustbin, the hose and the tap
Mr Fisher	Back to my toadstool and get a good nap
Mr Wheeler } **Mr Fisher**	Back to the life of a garden gnome Back to back In our back yard Back home.
Mr Wheeler **Mr Fisher** **Chips**	Holidays can't last for ever All good things must end they say Now our weekend trip is over So we must wend our way.

They start off

All	Back home
Mr Wheeler } **Mr Fisher**	To our back yard
All	Back home
Chips	It's time to blow
All	Back home
Mr Wheeler } **Mr Fisher**	Where we belong
All	Back home
Mr Wheeler } **Mr Fisher**	To the world we know Back to the Big Ones, the shed and the wall Back as though nothing had happened at all Back to the life of a garden gnome

All (*Chips*	Back to back
refering it to	In our back yard
the Gnomes)	Back home.

It is suggested that the characters proceed on their journey home by going down into the auditorium, with the House Lights up; this also takes the focus off the stage to accommodate the scene change. The following two verses should be sufficient for the journey through the auditorium

    Back home
    To our back yard
    Back home
    It's time to go
    Back home
    Where we belong
    Back home
    To the world we know
    Back to the dustbin, the hose and the tap
    Back to the toadstool and get a good nap
    Back to the life of a garden gnome
    Back to back
    In our back yard
    Back home.

    Back home
    To our back yard
    Back home
    It's time to blow
    Back home
    Where we belong
    Back home
    To the world we know
    Back to the Big Ones, the shed and the wall
    Back as though nothing had happened at all
    Back to the life of a garden gnome
    Back to back
    In our back yard
    Back home.

The characters reach the stage, on which the back yard set is now ready. The lights go up just downstage. The House Lights fade

    All cross the stage singing the following verse, and exit the other side

    Back home
    To our back yard
    Back home
    It's time to go
    Back home
    Where we belong
    Back home

Act 2, Scene 3

>   To the world we know
>   Back to the dustbin, the hose and the tap
>   Back to the toadstool and get a good nap
>   Back to the life of a garden gnome
>   Back to back
>   In our back yard
>   Back home

The heads of Mr Wheeler and Mr Fisher appear over the wall. They start climbing down, lowering the wheelbarrow, and helping Baby Duck down. Chips watches from the top of the wall

As they sing the lights very gradually increase

>   Back home
>   To our back yard
>   Back home
>   It's time to blow
>   Back home
>   Where we belong
>   Back home
>   To the world we know.

The next section is sung out of tempo, to accommodate action

>   Back where we started, climb over the wall
>   Mind how we go now, take care not to fall
>   Back to the life of a garden gnome
>   Back to back
>   In our back yard
>   Back home.
>
>   Back to the dustbin, the hose and the tap
>   Back to the toadstool and get a good nap
>   Back to the life of a garden gnome
>   Back to back
>   In our back yard
>   Back home.

During the final lines, Mr Fisher runs happily to his toadstool and climbs up. The Gnomes are back to back in their usual positions. Baby Duck watches; Chips stays up on the wall. It is now daylight

Mr Wheeler ⎫ Back to back
Mr Fisher ⎭ In our back yard
           Back home.

Scene 3

The Back Yard. Morning

Mr Wheeler Absence makes the heart grow fonder, Mr Fisher.
Mr Fisher Indeed, Mr Wheeler.

Mr Wheeler (*seeing Chips still on the wall*) Chips. Come down and see the shed.
Chips (*shy at invading their territory*) It's OK, Mr Wheeler, I'll just sus things out from up here.
Mr Wheeler As you wish. Fancy a drop of water?

He starts to arrange the hose, giving Chips the end. Baby Duck is subdued, wandering round. He stops at the dustbin. He quacks

Mr Fisher (*going to him*) It's all right, Fluffy Duck, we won't let the Big Ones throw you in there again. Come and see the shed. You can shelter there too...

They start towards the shed off-stage. Mr Wheeler goes to turn on the tap

Sudden noise stops everyone in their tracks. The Big Ones' car drives up. After a final rev. of the engine, it stops. Car doors slam.

The shadows of the Big Ones give a lighting change to heighten the tension

The Gnomes hurry to their original opening positions. If necessary, Mr Wheeler helps Mr Fisher up on to his toadstool, then returns to his wheelbarrow. They adopt their frozen positions. Baby Duck runs round, then stops behind the dustbin, hiding. Chips—not understanding what is going on—stands on the wall rooted to the spot

We hear the voices of the Big Ones, on their way to the back door

Mr Big One Unpack later. Let's have a nice cup of tea first.
Miss Big One Can I turn the telly on, Mum?
Mrs Big One All right, love.

There is the sound of the back door being unlocked

(*With a sigh*) It's always nice to get home.
Miss Big One Hey, Mum, look. On the wall.

Chips reacts

Mrs Big One Hello, puss. We haven't seen you before. Are you lost?
Mr Big One Looks a bit thin to me.
Miss Big One Can we give him some milk?
Mrs Big One Why not?
Miss Big One Come on. Puss, puss, puss. Want some milk?

Chips hesitates

It's all right, we won't hurt you.

Chips starts climbing down, using the hose if necessary

Good boy. Come on.

Chips goes towards the back door

Oh, Mum. He looks ever so hungry. Can we keep him?
Mrs Big One Well...

Act 2, Scene 3

Mr Big One Tell you what. We'll stick a note on the gate. And if nobody claims him, he can stay and live with us.

Chips looks happy. He turns to the Gnomes, who beam with pleasure, and maybe even nod encouragement

Chips exits

Baby Duck creeps out from behind the dustbin to see what is going on

Mrs Big One What's that by the dustbin?
Miss Big One It's my Baby Duck.
Mr Big One The one that didn't work? I thought you'd thrown it away.
Mrs Big One I *did* throw it away.
Mr Big One You must have missed. I'll pop it back in.

The Gnomes and Baby Duck look alarmed. In fright, Baby Duck scuttles out, waddling perfectly

Miss Big One Look! He's working again. He's all right!
Mrs Big One Well, I never.
Mr Big One You can't throw him away now.
Miss Big One I never wanted to in the first place! Come on, Baby Duck, come and meet our new pussycat.

Baby Duck smiles happily, looks at the Gnomes and waves. They smile back

Baby Duck exits

Mrs Big One Hello, Gnomes!

The Gnomes react

Mr Big One Dear old Gnomes. Brightening up the back yard as usual.
Mrs Big One I always like coming home because I know they'll be waiting to welcome us.
Mr Big One Funny. They're only stone, but they're really part of the family. Wouldn't be the same without them. I really must get that fish pond built for them, with some real fish in it.
Mrs Big One Come on, love, let's get the kettle on

The door slams. The Lights return to normal

The Gnomes look much moved

Mr Fisher (*after a pause*) You know, Mr Wheeler?
Mr Wheeler What, Mr Fisher?
Mr Fisher The Big Ones aren't so bad, really.
Mr Wheeler They're only human, Mr Fisher.
Mr Fisher Real fish in a real fishpond!
Mr Wheeler I bet *their* holiday wasn't as exciting as ours.
Mr Fisher We found our island.
Mr Wheeler We nearly got whacked.
Mr Fisher I did some real fishing.
Mr Wheeler Even my wheelbarrow came in handy. Doggy Dins. Fluffy Duck.

Mr Fisher And we managed to help two friends in distress.
Mr Wheeler The Code of the Gnomes!
Mr Fisher My life, Mr Wheeler, is not a wasted life after all.

          SONG 10a: **The Code Of The Gnomes** (Reprise)

Mr Fisher ⎫ **Mr Wheeler** ⎭	If Ever you're in danger or need a friend Be sure that we'll stick by you until the bitter end
Mr Wheeler	It's up to us
Mr Fisher	It's up to us
Mr Wheeler	It's up to us
Mr Fisher	It's up to us
Both	We won't wait Or hesitate Just put us to the test
Mr Wheeler	It's up to us
Mr Fisher	It's up to us
Mr Wheeler	It's up to us
Mr Fisher	It's up to us
Both	The Code of the Gnomes We do our best.

As the song ends, the two gnomes, nodding asleep, freeze into the positions in which they opened the play. The Lights fade to a Black-out as—

                    the CURTAIN falls

OPTIONAL CURTAIN CALL

The lights come up again, and the Gnomes are joined by Chips and Baby Duck

All We found our holiday island
Our holiday pie in the sky land
There was nothing to do
But enjoy doing nothing
There was nothing to do
But have fun

Securidog and Wacker run on and join in

Securidog } And
Wacker   } Now
You're
All Home
In our back yard
Back home
It's good to see
Our home
Where we belong
Back home
Is the place to be
Back to the dustbin, the hose and the tap
Back to the toadstool and get a good nap
Back to the life of a garden gnome
Back to back
In our back yard
Back home

We found our
Holiday island
Yours and my land
Pie in the sky land
Do or die land
Island in the sun
We found our
Holiday island
Yours and my land
Pie in the sky land
Do or die land
Island in the sun
We found our holiday island
Yours and my land

Pie in the sky land
Do or die land
Holiday, holiday,
Holiday, holiday,
Island in the sun.

CURTAIN

FURNITURE AND PROPERTY LIST

A cyclorama or back-drop of an urban skyline is visible throughout

ACT 1
Scene 1

On stage: Wall. *On it*: tap with attached hosepipe
Tubs of plants
Dustbin and lid
Toadstool
Fishing-rod with bell on top (for **Mr Fisher**)
Wheelbarrow (for **Mr Wheeler**)
Other dressing as desired
Off stage: Large screwdriver (**Mr Wheeler**)
Personal: **Baby Duck**: piece of fluff in key area

Scene 2

On stage: Upright part of street-lamp
Off stage: Wheelbarrow (**Mr Wheeler**)
Fishing-rod (**Mr Fisher**)
(*Note: these props are used by these characters for the rest of the play*)

Scene 3

On stage: Wire-netting fence and gate. *On fence and gate:* signs "KEEP OUT", "BEWARE OF THE GUARD DOG", "TRESPASSERS WILL BE PROSECUTED", Burglar alarm system with "BURGLAR ALARM" sign.
Above fence: "ADVENTURE PLAYGROUND" sign
Rubber tyre swing
Tunnel of pipe
Dog kennel. *On it*: "SECURIDOG" sign, rope for **Securidog**
"Doggy Dins" food bowl and food
Personal: **Securidog**: notebook and pencil

ACT 2
Scene 1

On stage: Pavement rostrum. *On it*: wall with "WET TAR" sign
Drain with grating
Patch of "wet tar"
Warning lantern
Red and white striped cones
Road works barrier and sign

Scene 2

Off stage: Traffic island truck. *On it*: two bollards, flashing Belisha beacon (**Stage Management**)

Towards the end of this scene, while the characters proceed on their journey through the auditorium, the traffic island truck is removed and the Back Yard set for Scene 3.

Scene 3

On stage: As ACT 1, Scene 1

LIGHTING PLOT

Property fittings required: warning lantern, flashing Belisha beacon

ACT 1 Scene 1
To open:	House Lights up	
Cue 1	After overture	(Page 1)
	Fade House Lights	
Cue 2	Door slams	(Page 1)
	Bring up general lighting—afternoon	
Cue 3	Back door opens	(Page 9)
	Dramatic lighting change, with optional shadow effect of the Big Ones	
Cue 4	Car drives off	(Page 9)
	Return to previous lighting	
Cue 5	**Gnomes** and **Baby Duck** disappear over wall	(Page 11)
	Fade to Black-out	

ACT 1 Scene 2
To open:	Dim lighting—dusk	
Cue 6	**Mr Fisher**: "It's getting quite dark."	(Page 13)
	Snap on spot to represent street-lamp	
Cue 7	**Gnomes** and **Baby Duck** say goodbye and start off towards audience	(Page 17)
	Dazzling light to represent car headlights	
Cue 8	**Gnomes** and **Baby Duck** set off again	(Page 17)
	Repeat Cue 7	
Cue 9	**Gnomes** and **Baby Duck** creep forward	(Page 17)
	Repeat Cue 7	
Cue 10	**Mr Wheeler**: "Thanks." (*They try again*)	(Page 17)
	Repeat Cue 7	
Cue 11	**Chips**: "Everybody stand up."	(Page 18)
	Bring up House Lights	
Cue 12	**Chips**: "You can sit down now."	(Page 20)
	Fade House Lights	
Cue 13	**Chips**, the **Gnomes** and **Baby Duck** cross the "road"	(Page 20)
	Fade to Black-out	

ACT 1 Scene 3
To open:	Dim evening light and street-lamp-type lighting	
Cue 14	**Mr Wheeler** and **Chips** crawl under gate	(Page 23)
	Focus lighting inside Adventure Playground	
Cue 15	**Securidog** crashes into wire fence	(Page 23)
	Flashing blue lights	
Cue 16	**Voice 2**: ". . . . whoever you are."	(Page 28)
	*Spot flashes round stage and comes to rest on **Securidog***	
Cue 17	**Securidog** gets in kennel	(Page 29)
	Snap off spot	
Cue 18	Car drives off	(Page 29)
	Return to previous lighting	

ACT 2 Scene 1

To open:	Dim evening light and street-lamp-type lighting over rostrum; flashing warning lantern on	
Cue 19	**Wacker** squirms in the tar like a stranded whale *Fade to Black-out*	(Page 40)

ACT 2 Scene 2

To open:	Follow-spot on **Chips** and the others as they move into the auditorium. *Optional*: bring up House Lights	
Cue 20	When ready *Fade follow-spot and/or House Lights; bring up dawn lighting on stage*	(Page 40)
Cue 21	**Mr Fisher**: "What are we waiting for?" (*He steps forward*) *Dazzling light to represent car headlights*	(Page 41)
Cue 22	**Chips**: "Everybody up!" *Bring up House Lights*	(Page 41)
Cue 23	**Chips**: "You can sit down now." *Fade House Lights*	(Page 41)
Cue 24	**Chips**: "Ah. Water." (*He considers*) *Fade lighting slightly, with optional rain effect*	(Page 43)
Cue 25	At end of SONG 9b *Fade rain effect (if used); increase general lighting—early morning*	(Page 43)
Cue 26	As **Chips** and the others move into auditorium *Bring up House Lights; fade lighting on stage*	(Page 46)
Cue 27	**Chips** and the others reach the stage *Bring up lights downstage; fade House Lights*	(Page 46)
Cue 28	**Mr Wheeler** and **Mr Fisher** climb down over wall *Start gradual increase in general lighting—up to daylight*	(Page 47)

ACT 2 Scene 3

To open:	Daylight	
Cue 29	Car doors slam *Dramatic lighting change, with shadow effect of the **Big Ones***	(Page 48)
Cue 30	**Mrs Big One**: " ... let's get that kettle on." *Return to opening lighting*	(Page 49)
Cue 31	SONG 10a ends and **gnomes** freeze *Fade to Black-out*	(Page 50)
Cue 32	(*optional*) When ready *Bring up general lighting for Curtain Call*	(Page 51)

EFFECTS PLOT

ACT 1

Cue 1	House Lights fade *Start* **Big Ones'** *tape: sound effects and voices as in text pages*	(Page 1)
Cue 2	**Mr Wheeler** turns **Baby Duck's** key *Ratchet noises*	(Page 6)
Cue 3	**Mr Wheeler** turns **Baby Duck's** key *Ratchet noises*	(Page 6)
Cue 4	As the **Gnomes** and **Baby Duck** dance at the end of SONG 2 *Start* **Big Ones'** *tape: sound effects and voices as in text pages*	(Page 9)
Cue 5	**Mr Wheeler** turns **Baby Duck's** key *Ratchet noises*	(Page 14)
Cue 6	**Gnomes** and **Baby Duck** say goodbye and start off towards audience *Car roars past*	(Page 17)
Cue 7	**Gnomes** and **Baby Duck** set off again *Repeat Cue 6*	(Page 17)
Cue 8	**Mr Wheeler**: "Come on, Mr Fisher." *Repeat Cue 6*	(Page 17)
Cue 9	**Mr Wheeler**: "Thanks." (*They try again*) *Repeat Cue 6*	(Page 17)
Cue 10	**Securidog** crashes into wire fence *Start* **Police** *tape: sound effects and voices as in text pages*	(Page 28)

ACT 2

Cue 11	(*optional*) As Curtain rises *Clock chimes 2 a.m.*	(Page 30)
Cue 12	**Chips** turns **Baby Duck's** key *Ratchet noises*	(Page 31)
Cue 13	**Baby Duck** presses **Wacker's** switch *Noise of pneumatic engine starting up*	(Page 33)
Cue 14	**Wacker** prepares to jump on **Baby Duck** *Engine revs up to crescendo; fade as* **Wacker** *lands on road*	(Page 35)
Cue 15	**Mr Wheeler** turns **Baby Duck's** key *Ratchet noises*	(Page 35)
Cue 16	**Wacker** prepares to jump on the Gnomes in the tar *Engine revs up to crescendo*	(Page 36)
Cue 17	**Chips** turns off **Wacker's** switch *Engine runs down*	(Page 37)
Cue 18	**Mr Wheeler** turns **Baby Duck's** key *Ratchet noises*	(Page 39)
Cue 19	**Chips** accidentally hits **Wacker's** switch *Noise of pneumatic engine starting up*	(Page 39)

Cue 20	**Mr Fisher**: "What are we waiting for?" (*He steps forward*)	(Page 41)
	Car roars past	
Cue 21	**Chips**: "Ah. Water." (*He considers*)	(Page 43)
	Clap of thunder, followed by rain effect	
Cue 22	At end of SONG 9b	(Page 43)
	Fade rain effect	
Cue 23	**Mr Wheeler** goes to turn on tap	(Page 48)
	Start Big Ones' tape: sound effects and voices as in text pages	

Printed in Great Britain by Butler & Tanner Ltd, Frome and London

www.ingramcontent.com/pod-product-compliance
Ingram Content Group UK Ltd.
Pitfield, Milton Keynes, MK11 3LW, UK
UKHW021847210426
5322IPUK00022B/509